AF395928

WALLS OF ARAN

SEAN SCULLY **WALLS OF ARAN**

INTRODUCTION BY COLM TÓIBÍN

AFTERWORD BY SEAN SCULLY

73 illustrations

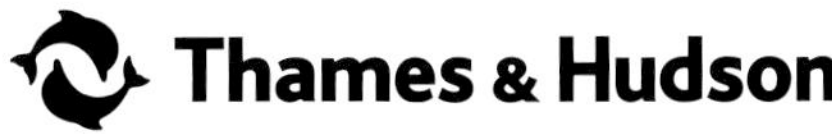

Thames & Hudson

Sean Scully is a world-renowned, Irish-born abstract artist who has had major museum exhibitions across Europe and the United States, and his works can be found in many important public and private collections. He has travelled to Aran regularly over a number of years.

Colm Tóibín is an award-winning author, a journalist and critic, and professor at Columbia University. His novels include *The Master, Brooklyn, The Testament of Mary* and *Nora Webster*. Among his non-fiction are *Bad Blood; New Ways to Kill Your Mother; Mad, Bad, Dangerous to Know*; and, as editor, *The Penguin Book of Irish Fiction*.

CONTENTS

COLM TÓIBÍN: ISLAND

1

I phoned from Spiddal at half past three to check that I was booked on the four o'clock flight to Inis Meáin and to say that I hoped I would be in time for it.

'There's bad weather', the man at the airport said. There was a calmness and resignation in his tone, a politeness verging on dry good-humour. 'Take your time', he said. 'There is no need to hurry at all. We won't be travelling anywhere for a while.'

'So I'll have a minute to stop at the cash machine in Spiddal?' I asked.

'We'll be still here, I'd say, when you come', he replied.

For the previous four hours, as I drove west from Dublin, the rain becoming more intense and the traffic in the small towns more chaotic, I had been so frantic to make the last plane of the day on time – the journey to the island would take a mere seven minutes – that I had put no thought at all into what it would be like when I got there, how different the days there would be, how empty and still and silent. The man's voice, the effortless charm he put into making the strong hint that there might not be a plane at all because of the weather, made me slow down for a second.

I was moving into a world of nature governed by wind and weather, sharp and soft lines of horizon, disappearing perspectives, high skies and great banks of cloud, and a world of people governed by careful politeness, watchful slow glances, and deliberate understatement.

In the small airport all the luggage was piled up and ready to be taken onto the planes; the waiting room was full of people with bookings for the last flight of the day to Árainn, or Inis Mór, the largest island, Inis Oírr, the smallest one, or Inis Meáin, the one in the middle. On our side, the rain seemed to be easing and there was almost brightness in the western sky, the sky over the sea, but this meant nothing as word came that on the islands themselves, the three unprotected islands open to the ferocity of the Atlantic winds, the weather had deteriorated. There would be no more flights. Anyone wanting to travel would have to get the ferries from Rosaveel, about six miles to the north. It would, everyone agreed, be a rough crossing. We carried our luggage out to the bus to take us to the ferry.

There were hardly any tourists going to Inis Meáin that evening; a young American woman who could speak Irish and play the uileann pipes and a couple and their two young children who said that they had been coming every year seemed to be the only outsiders. The rest were islanders, or people going to Inis Oírr. Very few of the passengers seemed comfortable as the boat got ready to leave the shore. They sat in the lounge as though preparing for an ordeal. As the boat moved off a few of us stayed on the bottom deck, hands firmly on the rails, looking at the rain-washed land and the fierce grey sea, the water full of its own angry power, but oddly calm and flat, like something held down, contained, but swelling, ready to do its worst at any moment, waiting to be provoked.

As we moved out of the harbour things changed. The boat was not moving through the waves as much as lunging against them; soon we had to move into the doorways and hold tight as sea water washed across the deck every time we inched forward. Behind us, travelling low over the waves, a rescue helicopter came, the noise of the propellers adding to the drama. They were on a training mission, needing to acquaint themselves with weather at its worst. In the lounge people's faces were turning green. It was a perfect day for seasickness.

I stood in the doorway watching the water churning in the wake of the boat. The sea around us seemed steeped in its own greyness and grimness. There was a fierce white rush of disturbance as the boat pushed through the waves, and then a beautiful light green appeared fleetingly in the water, almost turquoise in the undertow, as the water settled again. I concentrated on this colour which was elusive and then vivid and then thrown under again, surfacing once more as though struggling to be recognized. I did not mind the rolling of the boat, or being regularly soaked in spray. I watched for this colour in the embattled water and thought that if this is all I see during my time on the island, it will be enough. I do not need anything more.

I came to the Aran Islands first in September 1977, when there were no proper piers on Inis Oírr and Inis Meáin, when an unwieldy ship called the *Naomh Éanna* from Galway Harbour was the main means of transport. On a calm Sunday, I remember, it anchored off the smallest island and men came out in currachs, small traditional fishing boats; each person had to be lowered from the large boat down into the small one, each piece of luggage too, just as we would have to be hauled back up on our return. Animals, too, would have to be hauled up and down in slings. The harbour at Inis Oírr was more sheltered than the one at Inis Meáin, boats could come in and out from Doolin in County Clare. But only the *Naomh Éanna* serviced the middle island and it could only anchor on a very

calm day. This meant that the middle island remained the most cut off, the least
visited, the most mysterious, the island where timelessness, such as it was,
held most sway.

Over the next decade access improved, a plane service was added, the *Naomh
Éanna* taken out of use, faster boats from the harbour at Rosaveel outside Galway
began to service the islands. It became possible and popular in the summer to do day
trips to Árainn and to Inis Oírr. I stayed a few days on the big island four or five times,
renting a bicycle, making my way to the great cliffs over the Atlantic, or the small
beautiful beaches. Once I flew to Árainn, stayed for a couple of days, then got a fishing
boat to take me to Inis Oírr and then travelled from there to Doolin on the mainland.
We stopped at Inis Meáin for only one moment, but I remained on the boat. In all
those years I never once put my foot on the middle island. I was saving it up.

What I remember most vividly from those years were the following images:
a Sunday after mass in the pub in Inis Oírr in 1977 and an old man starting to sing,
the voice rich and confident, a song in Irish that I did not know, a quietness
gathering around him until there was complete silence in the bar as he sang verse
after verse of a love song with no chorus, adding to the narrative, as far as I could
make out, further causes for lament.

And in 1982, I remember discovering the Black Fort on Árainn for the first time, standing on the massive cut rocks watching the waves crash below, spending an hour or two alone there on a summer Sunday. And maybe four or five years later, also on my own, coming off the boat from Rosaveel on a Saturday evening and passing the pub on the way to the bed and breakfast I had booked and noticing the writer Breandán Ó hEithir, who was from the island, in the pub and spending two evenings in his company. Although he made everything on the big island seem complex, not dreamy at all or romantic, funny at times yet worthy of detailed attention, he grew silent at the mention of the middle island, saying it was different and always had been. He spoke to me that day about Tim Robinson, a writer and mapmaker, who had come to live on the island and who had learned the language not only of the people, but of every stone and system, and written a number of superb books on islands.

And four or five years after that, I remember speeding back to the mainland at Rosaveel on a boat one Sunday evening in the high summer, not a cloud in the sky, after a few days of magnificent weather, sitting at the back of the boat, looking forward to getting back to Galway, watching the sun over the calm, clear water.

But in all those years I kept away from the middle island. Once, in a shop in Galway, the owner showed me a pullover made there. It was knitted in the traditional Aran style, with much elaborate patterning, but it was made from alpaca wool. It was expensive and utterly beautiful. It bore the label Inis Meáin and suggested that change there was being forged with flair and originality. It added to the mystery of the middle island.

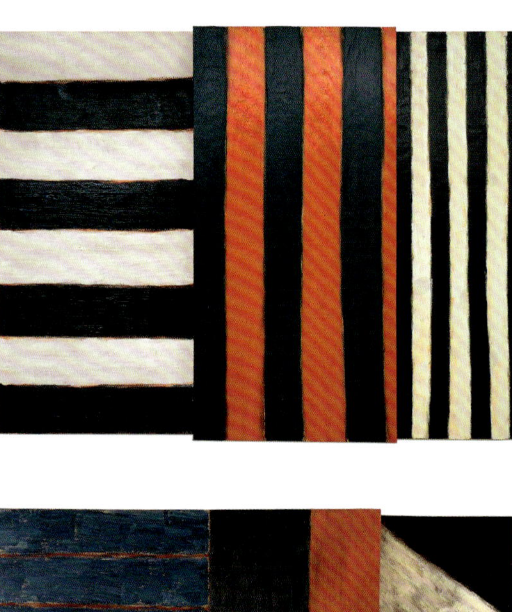

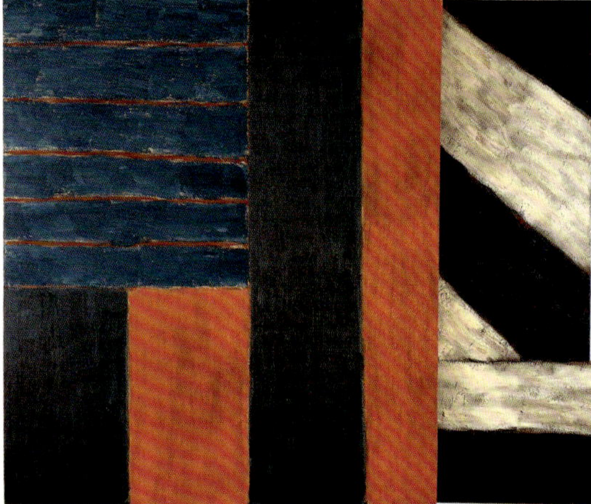

Inis Mór

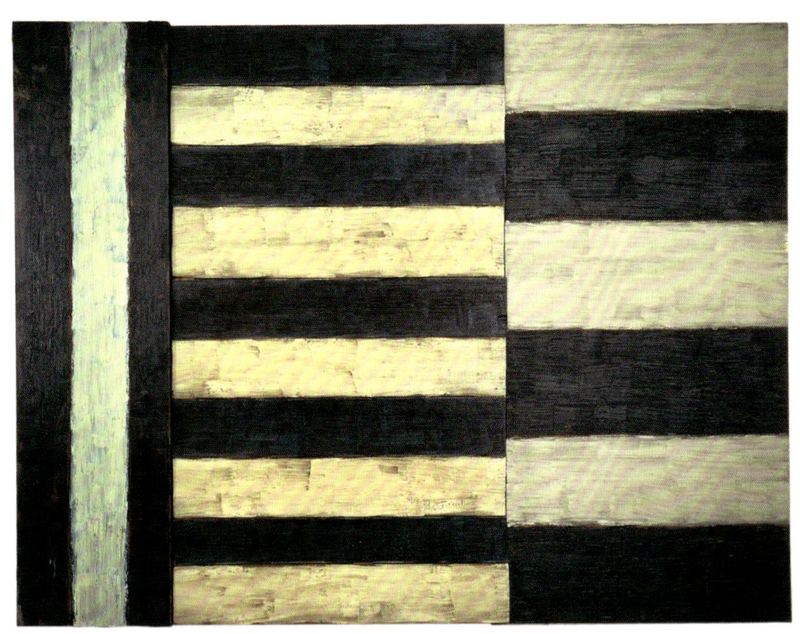

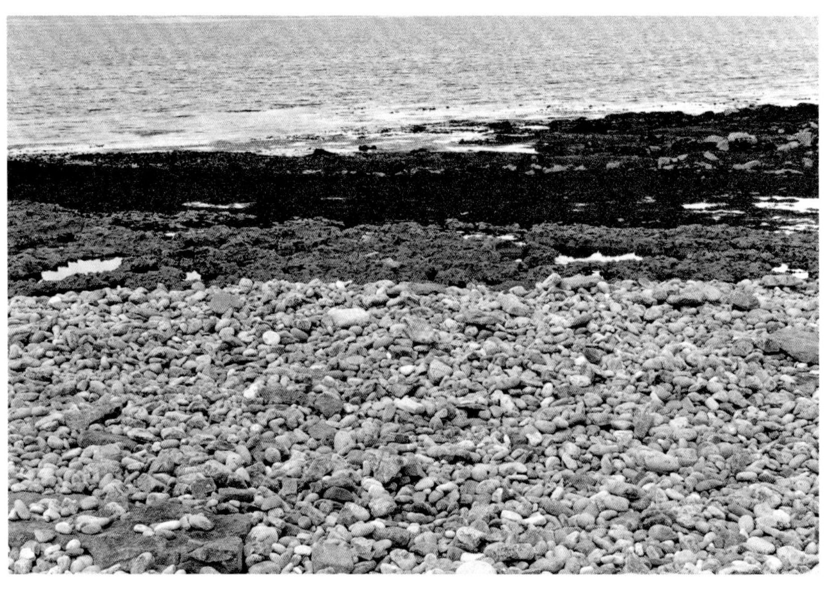
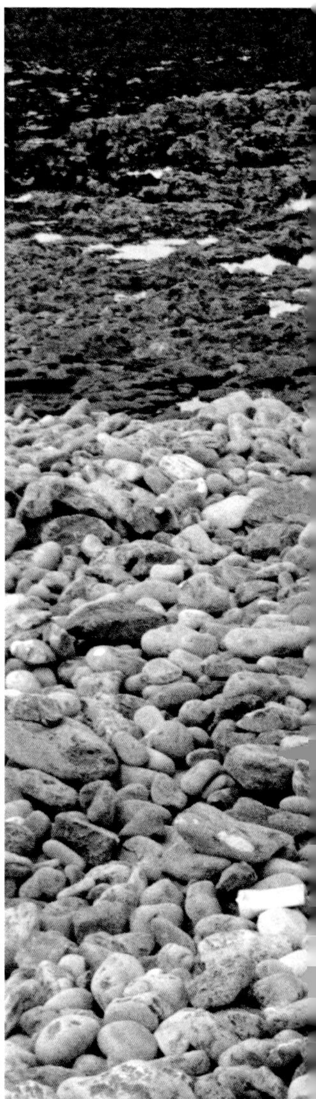

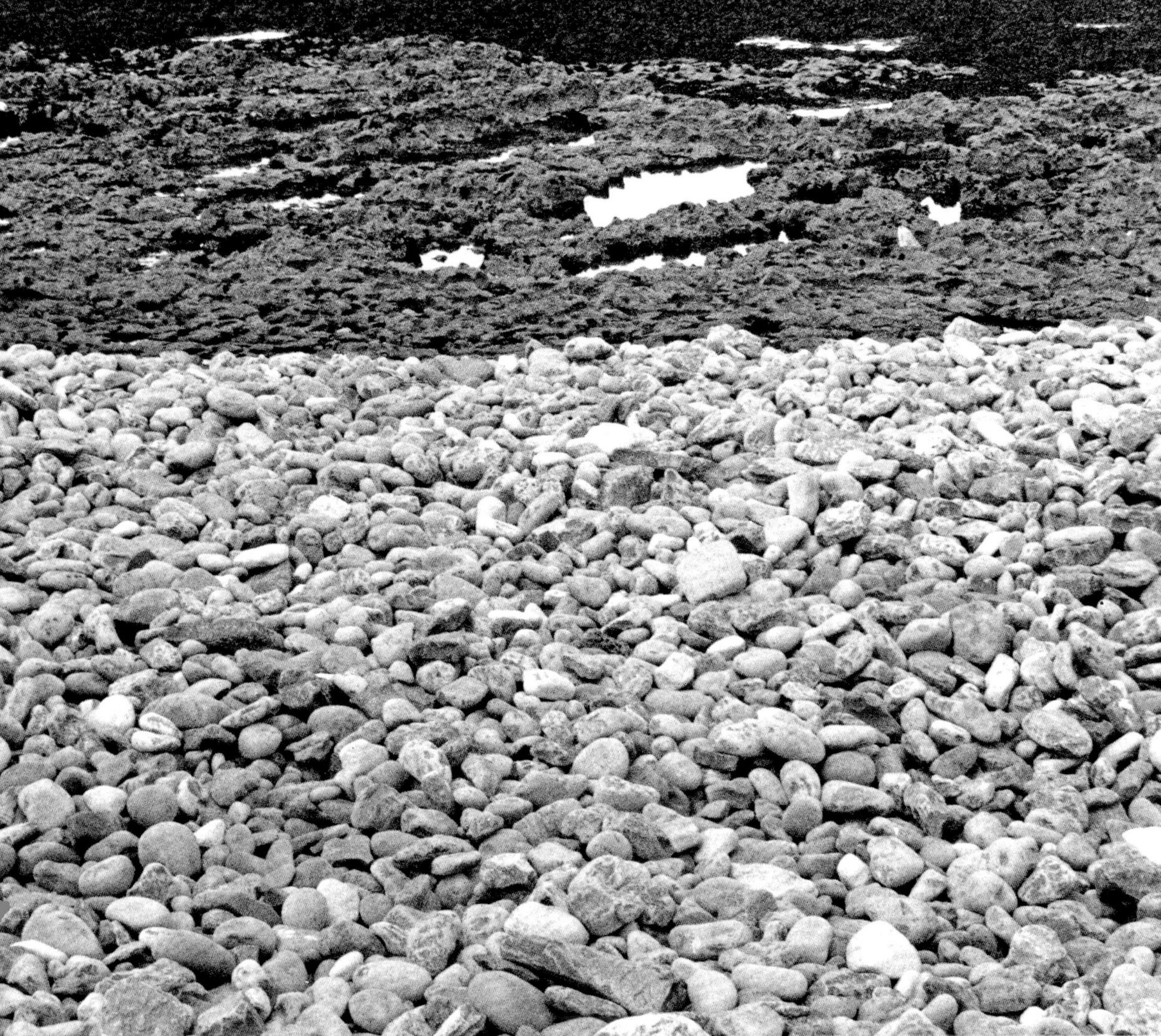

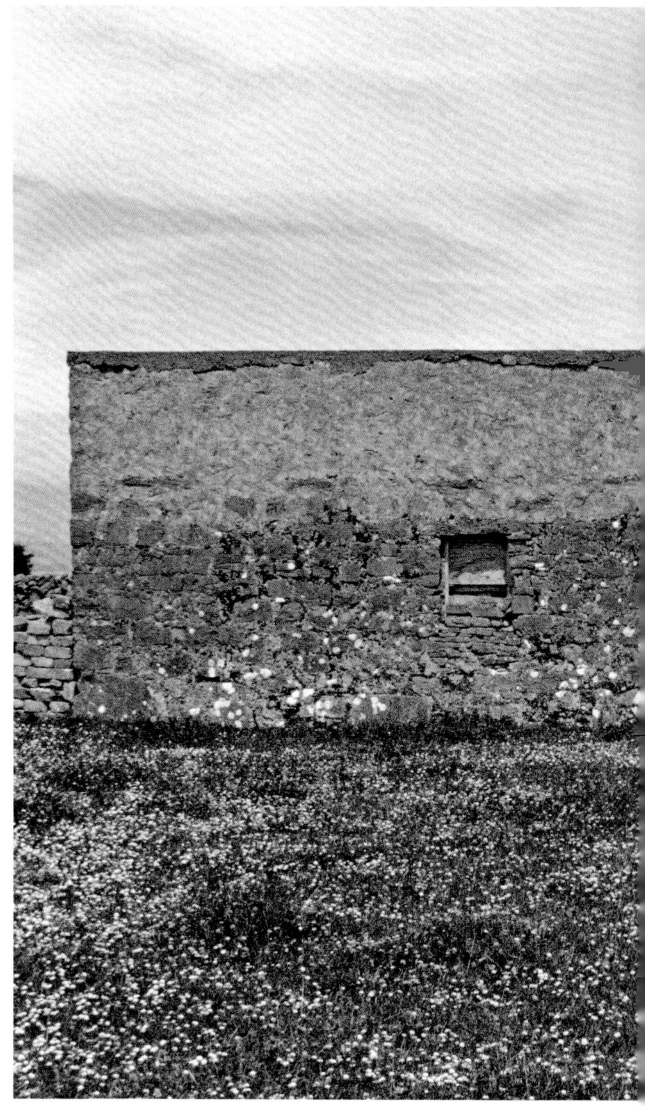

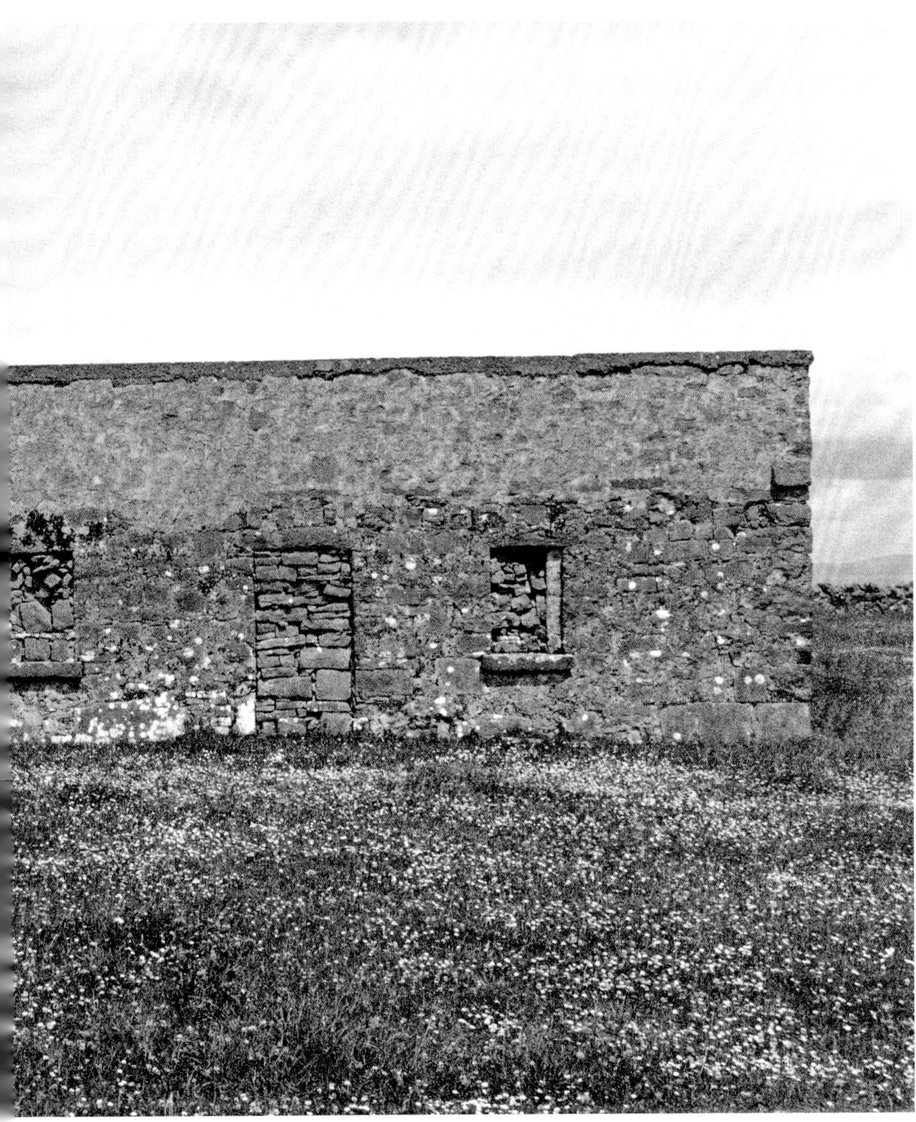

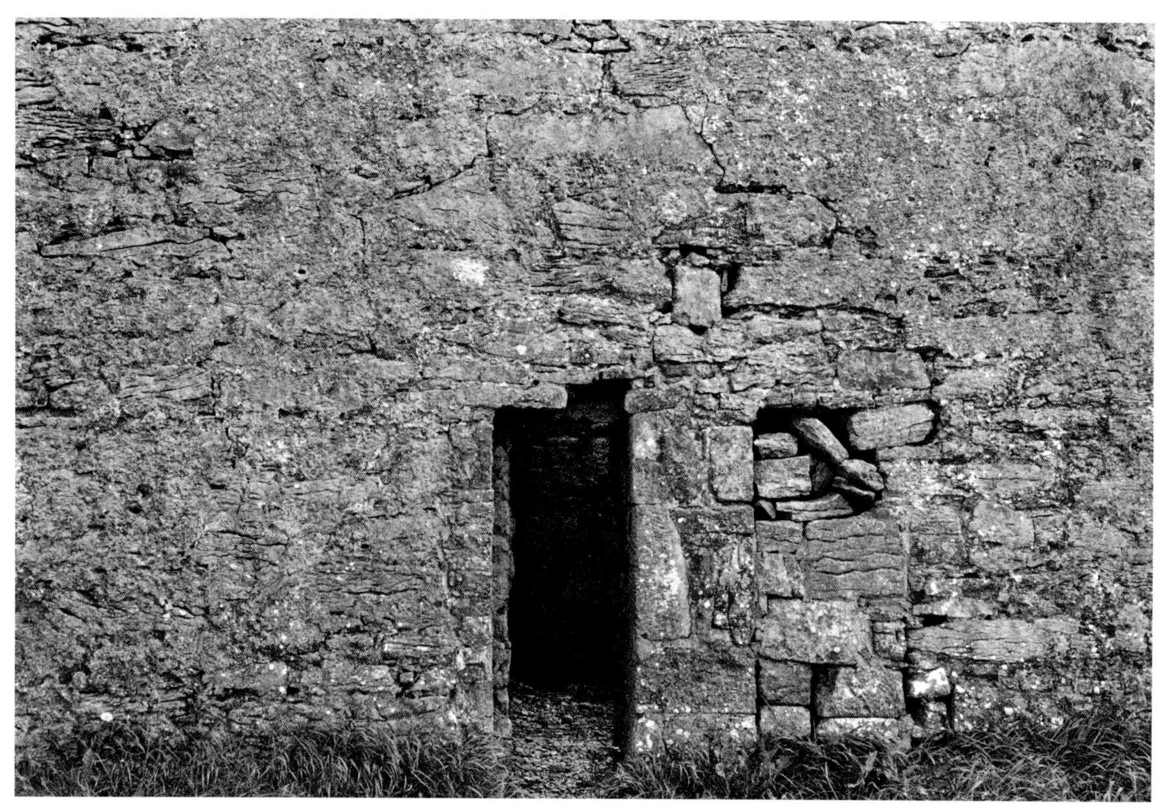

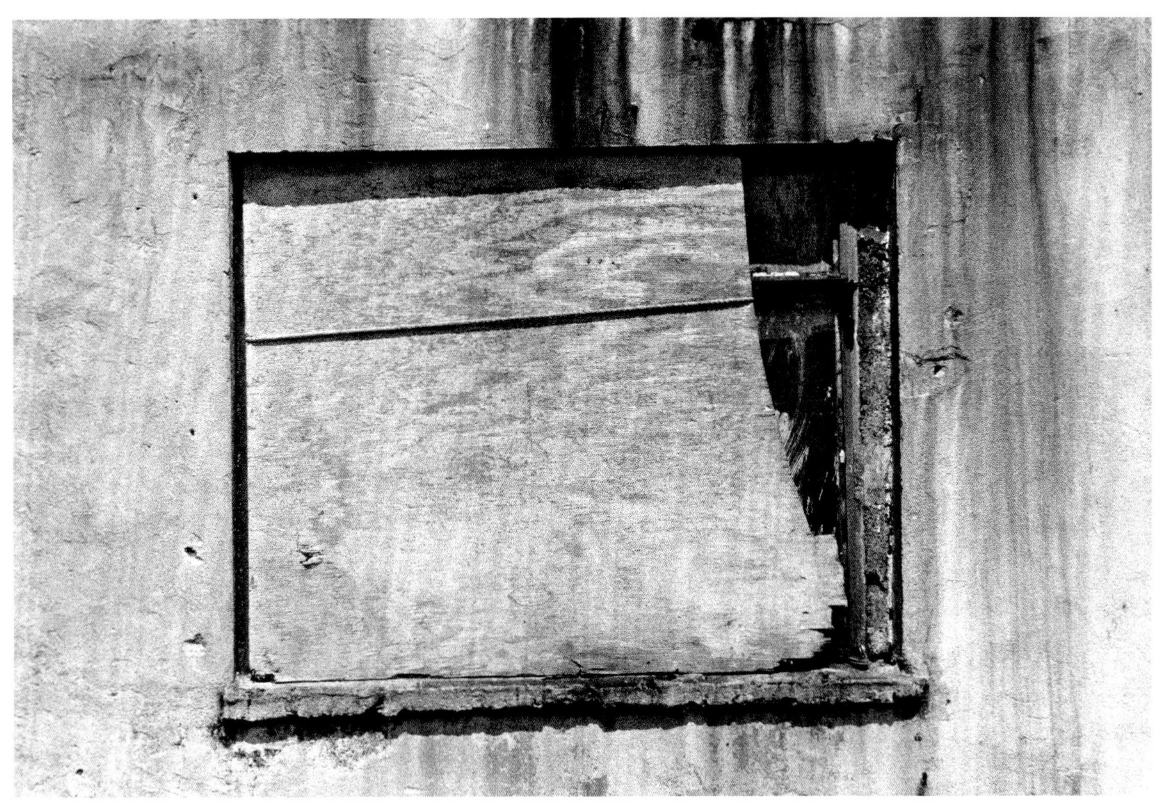

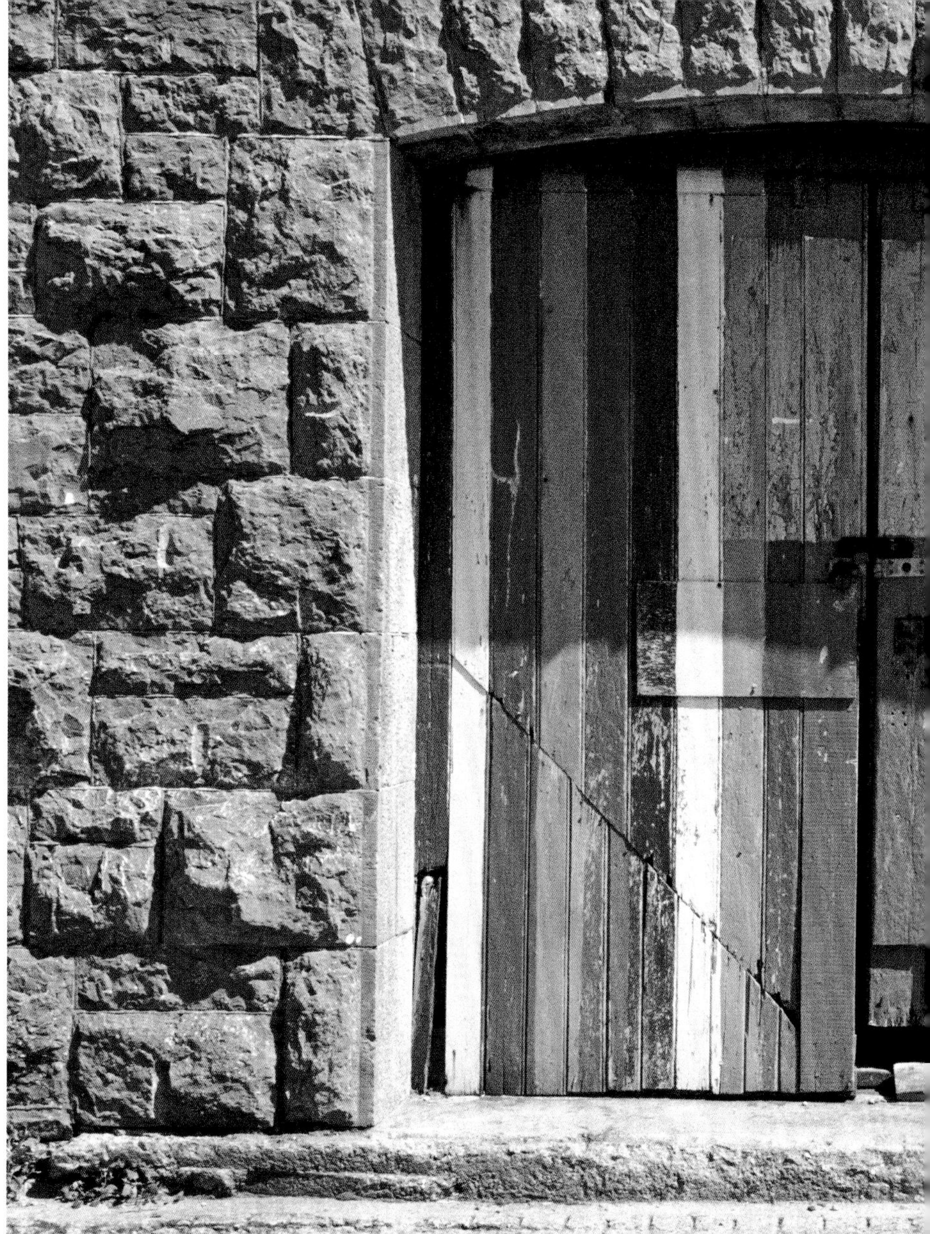

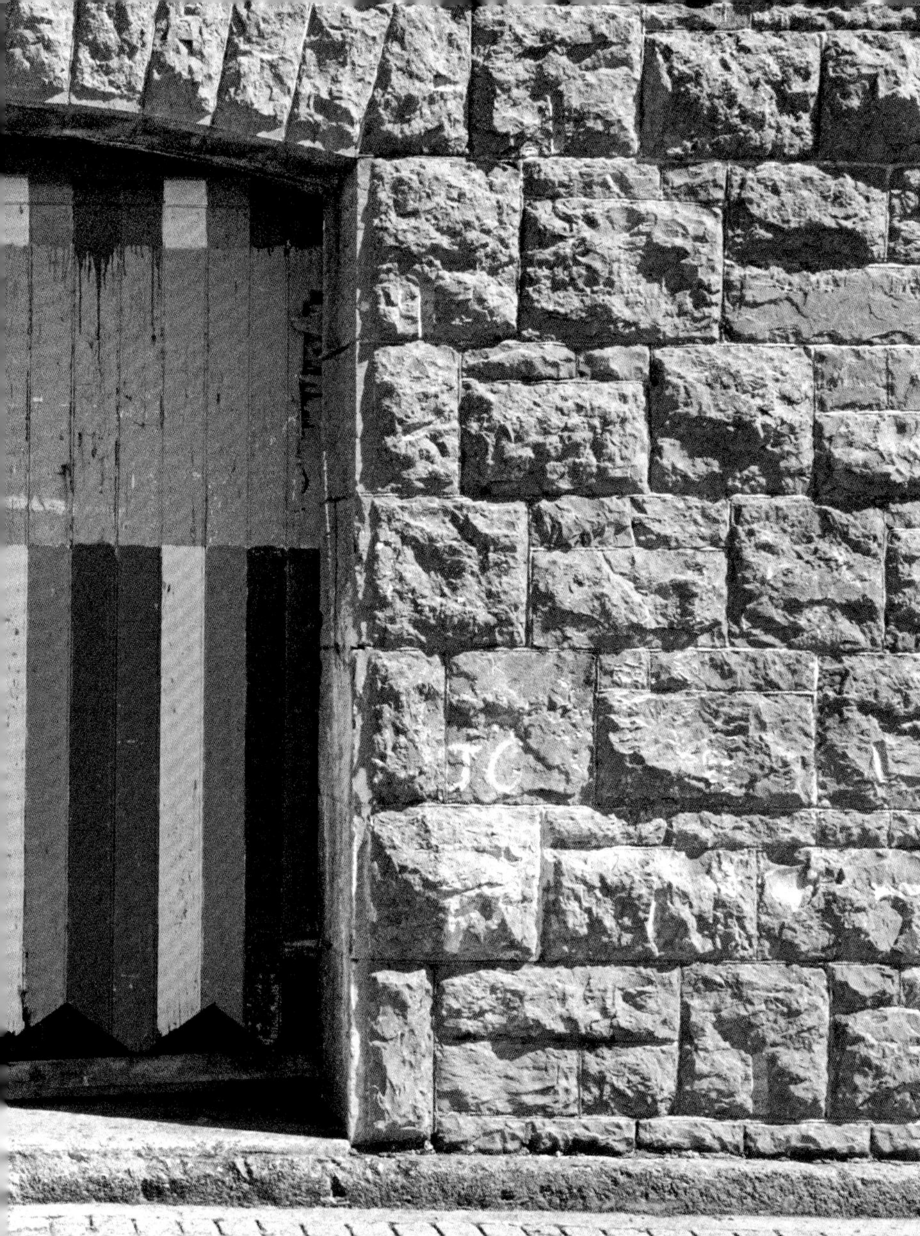

2

The mystery of all the islands came not only from their remoteness and the strangeness of the landscape, but from the people. Part of the pleasure of spending two days with Breandán Ó hEithir and talking about the islands was his interest in dispelling the idea that the islanders were different. He made their speaking Irish seem natural and the work they did seem normal, not part of any great repository of ancient lore or systems of belief that required genuflection. He remembered a group of doctors and sociologists, intent on finding a great remote society on the islands, coming to take blood samples and measure the size of the schoolchildren's heads. He loved the fact that the islanders' blood-group pattern turned out to be similar to that of northern England, where people of Gaelic and Saxon origin had also intermingled.

But the early visitors to the islands, who wrote the first books and articles, and established the sense of value in the islanders' otherness, were intent on finding simplicity and nobility in the character of the people they met. George Petrie, the antiquarian who visited the island first in 1822, for example wrote: 'The Araners are remarkable for fine intellect and deep sensibility…. Those whom chance has led to their hospitable shores … admire their simple virtues … much of their superiority must be attributed to their remote insular situation.'

In 1927, the writer Liam O'Flaherty, like his nephew Breandán Ó hEithir a native of the largest of the Aran islands, found himself on an island off county Donegal. He wrote to his London publisher: 'Life here is simpler than on my island. The people are less intelligent, and they have practically no imagination. Their speech is abrupt, considered and very realist. They are more straightforward, more kindly and less astute than my people. My people … are all born aristocrats with all the vices of aristocracy and some of its virtues…. There are no ruins here, no churches, forts or works of art as in my island. It is a serf of a place.'

Yet in the same year, when he found himself back on the island, O'Flaherty felt that the power of the Aran Islands came from the landscape rather than the people. He wrote to his publisher: 'It was splendid on Aran. The island has the character and personality of a mute God. One is awed in its presence, breathing its air. Over it broods an overwhelming sense of great, noble tragedy. The Greeks would have liked it. The people are sadly inferior to the island itself. But the sea birds are almost worthy of it. The great cormorants thrilled me. And while fishing on the brink of a rock, a great bull seal rose from the sea in front of me. He looked at me with brutal, drunken eyes and then dived.'

'Aran, it is said,' James Joyce wrote in 1912, 'is the strangest place in the world.' In his story 'The Dead', it is where Miss Ivors and her friends would go to refind the real Ireland. This wild landscape and the people who inhabited it attracted scholars and writers throughout the nineteenth century, including Sir William Wilde, father of the playwright, the naturalist Robert Lloyd Praeger, the poet W. B. Yeats and the revolutionaries Patrick Pearse and Thomas MacDonagh. In 1893 Lady Gregory, the founder with Yeats of the Irish National Theatre, came to the islands and stayed in a cottage on Inis Oírr. Five years later, when she went back, John Millington Synge was also on the island. 'I first saw him', she later wrote, 'in the North Island of Aran. I was staying there, gathering folklore, talking to the people, and felt a real pang of indignation when I passed another outsider walking here and there, talking also to the people. I was jealous of not being alone on the island among the fishers and seaweed gatherers. I did not speak to the stranger nor was he inclined to speak to me. He also looked on me as an intruder.'

Synge's *The Aran Islands* was first published in 1907. He wrote in his notebook: 'I cannot say it too often, the supreme interest of the island lies in the strange concord that exists between the people and the impersonal limited but powerful impulses of the nature that is round them.' He opened his book with a wonderful plain sentence: 'I am in Aranmor, sitting over a turf fire, listening to a murmur of Gaelic that is rising from a little public house under my room.' After fives pages, however, he moved to Inis Meáin. 'In spite of the charm of my teacher, the old blind man I met the day of my arrival, I have decided to move on to Inishmaan, where Gaelic is more generally used, and the life is perhaps the most primitive that is left in Europe.' 'This attribution', Tim Robinson has written, 'of a particular degree of Gaelic purity to the middle island was first made by [George] Petrie (1790–1866), who thought that the morals of the big island had been contaminated by people introduced to build the lighthouse in 1818, and those of Inis Oírr by its proximity to the Clare coast.'

Synge's book, when I read it first, seemed too clumsy and sketchy and artless, but over the years I have come to love it for its clarity and the beauty of its sentences. It comes, like the music of Sibelius, in a number of cold tones, reverting all the time to the original rhythms of its opening notes. In his book Synge repeats stories he is told using fresh dialogue and many flourishes and then when the story is finished, he reverts to his own style: 'A week of sweeping fogs has passed over and given me a strange sense of exile and desolation. I walk around the island nearly every day, yet I can see nothing anywhere but a mass of wet rock, a strip of surf, and then a tumult of waves.' He was the doomed genius, fresh from Paris, melancholy, solitary, overeducated, exhausted. He loved the wildness of Inis Meáin, the manners of the islanders, the beauty of the young women. He brought a camera and took photographs of the people; his own descriptions of his solitary journeys as a walker in changeable weather have a lovely detailed texture, single snapshots of himself alone, away from things. 'As I lie here hour after hour, I seem to enter into the wild pastimes of the cliff, and to become a companion of the cormorants and crows.' On a later visit, he wrote: 'This year I see a darker side of life in the islands. The sun seldom shines, and day after day a cold south-western wind blows over the cliffs, bringing up showers of hail and dense masses of cloud.'

As a playwright, he dramatized wildness of expression and attitude, independence of spirit. He found a poetic language of exuberance and wit. In his plays he explored the part of himself that was apparent to no one, least of all the reader who followed him on his strange journeys along the edges of Inis Meáin. ('There has been a storm for the last twenty-four hours, and I have been wandering the cliffs till my hair is stiff with salt.') But he wrote, too, about evictions on the islands, the creation of new fields from fields of rock and the plight of the islanders who have no proper harbour, where animals have to be rowed out in a currach to a hooker, a big traditional sailing boat, anchored eighty yards from the shore: 'Each bullock was caught in its turn and girded with a sling of rope by which it could be hoisted on board. Another rope was fastened to the horns and passed out to a man in the stern of the currach. Then the animal was forced down through the surf and out of its depth before it had much time to struggle. Once fairly swimming, it was towed out to the hooker and dragged on board in a half-drowned condition.'

He also wrote about a burial on Inis Meáin. 'While the grave was being opened the women sat down among the flat tombstones, bordered with a pale fringe of early bracken, and began the wild keen, or crying for the dead. Each old woman, as she took her turn in the leading recitative, seemed possessed for the moment with a profound ecstasy of grief, swaying to and fro, and bending her forehead to the stone before her, while she called out to the dead with a perpetually recurring chant of sobs.... In Inishmaan one is forced to believe in a sympathy between man and nature, and at this moment when the thunder sounded a death-peal of extraordinary grandeur above the voices of the women, I could see the faces near me stiff and drawn with emotion.'

Later in the book, Synge wrote an extraordinary description of the burial of a young man who had been drowned. As the grave was prepared, 'a number of blackened boards and pieces of bone had been thrown up with the clay, a skull was lifted out and placed on a gravestone'. A woman carried it away by herself and began to cradle it – 'it was the skull of her own mother'. As the coffin was ready to be lowered into the ground, Synge watched the scenes of lamentation: 'The young women were nearly lying among the stones, worn out with their passion of grief, yet raising themselves every few moments to beat with magnificent gestures on the boards of the coffin.') Synge made his play *Riders to the Sea* out of this scene. The play was first performed in 1904. Tim Robinson, in his magnificent introduction to Synge's book about the islands, remarks that 'Aran must have been long associated in the public mind with death by drowning.' Robinson cites Petrie's tale of 'an old Aran woman still grieving for her son lost to the sea, [Frederic] Burton's painting "The Aran Fisherman's Drowned Child"' (exhibited at the Royal Hibernian Academy in 1841, and circulated widely as an engraving), the heroine's drowning in Emily Lawless's 'Grania: The Story of an Island', published in 1892, among the many accounts.

But anyone who spends any time on the islands hears haunting stories about drownings and the grieving parents looking out to sea watching for the dead body, or parts of the body, to turn up on the tides, people waiting for their son to be identified and be buried. Synge visited the island after the events of December 1899, described by Tim Robinson: 'On the evening of the 28th of December, 1899, a number of fishermen were sleeping in their boats at anchor in the bay of Cill Éinne, in readiness for an early start the next morning, when a storm struck from the north. Their boats were smashed on the shore, and four men drowned.'

Robinson remarks also on the way in which in *Riders to the Sea* 'the action … is always on the point of condensing into ritual … North, south, east and west are so compulsively evoked as every change of wind and tide brings in a new anxiety or despair, that the island itself seethes in a doomful infusion of the compass rose. The elegiac rhythms of Synge's dialogue are those inherent in the English of native Irish speakers.'

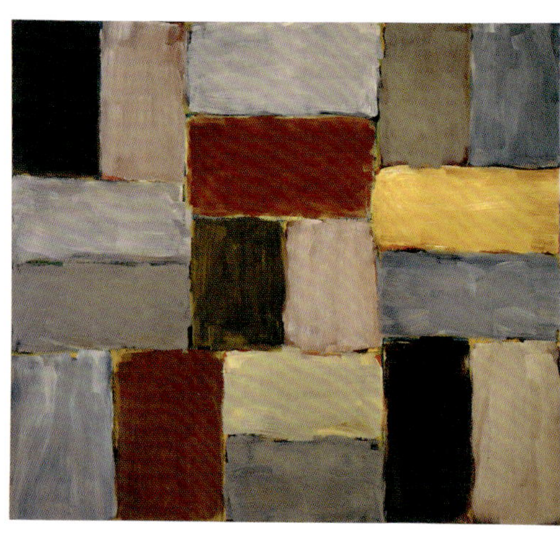

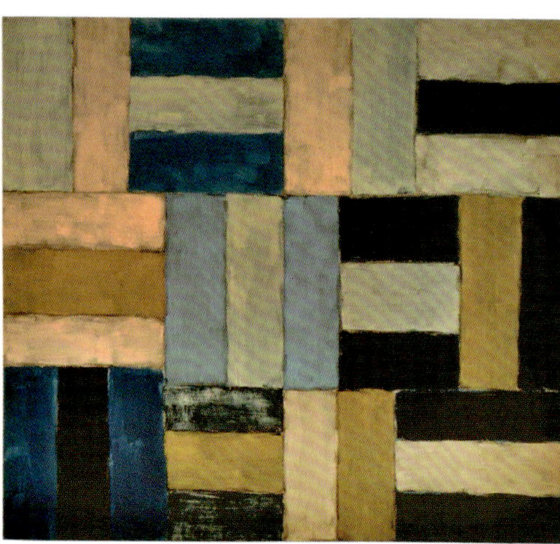

Inis Oírr

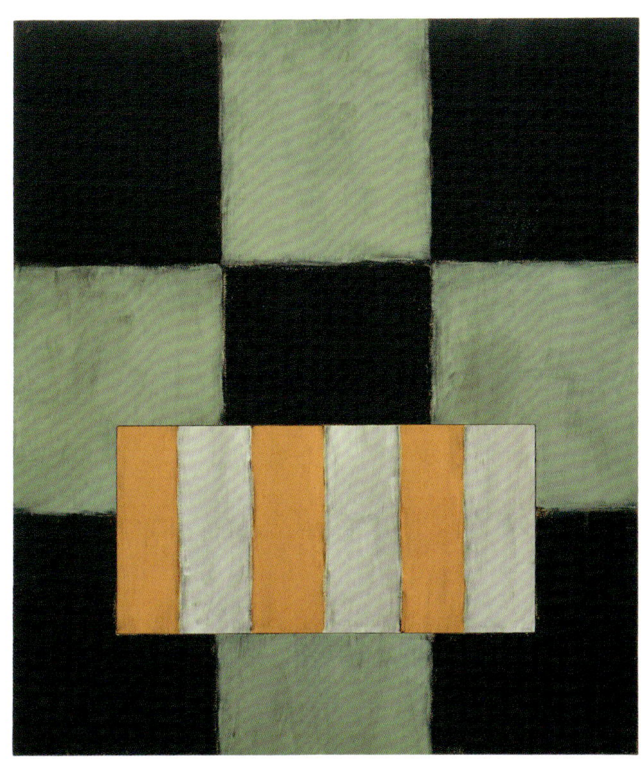

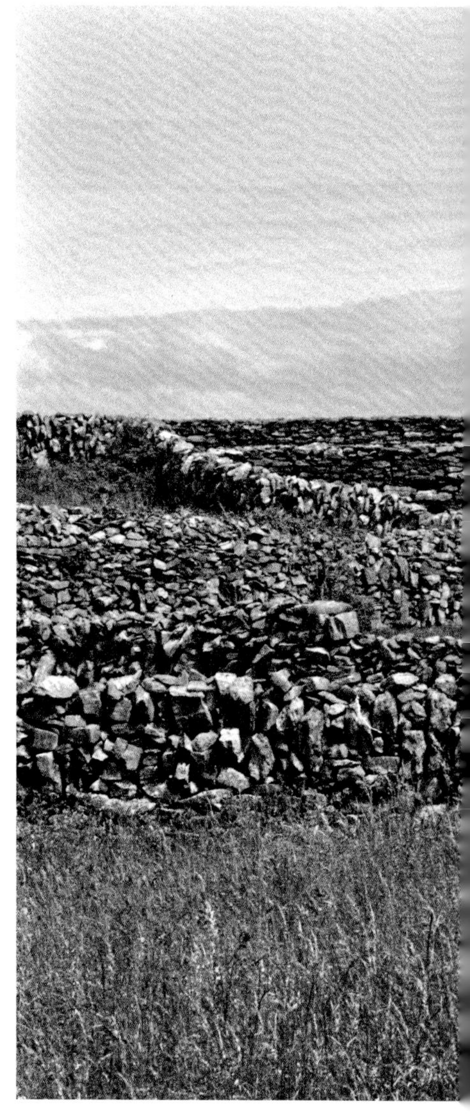

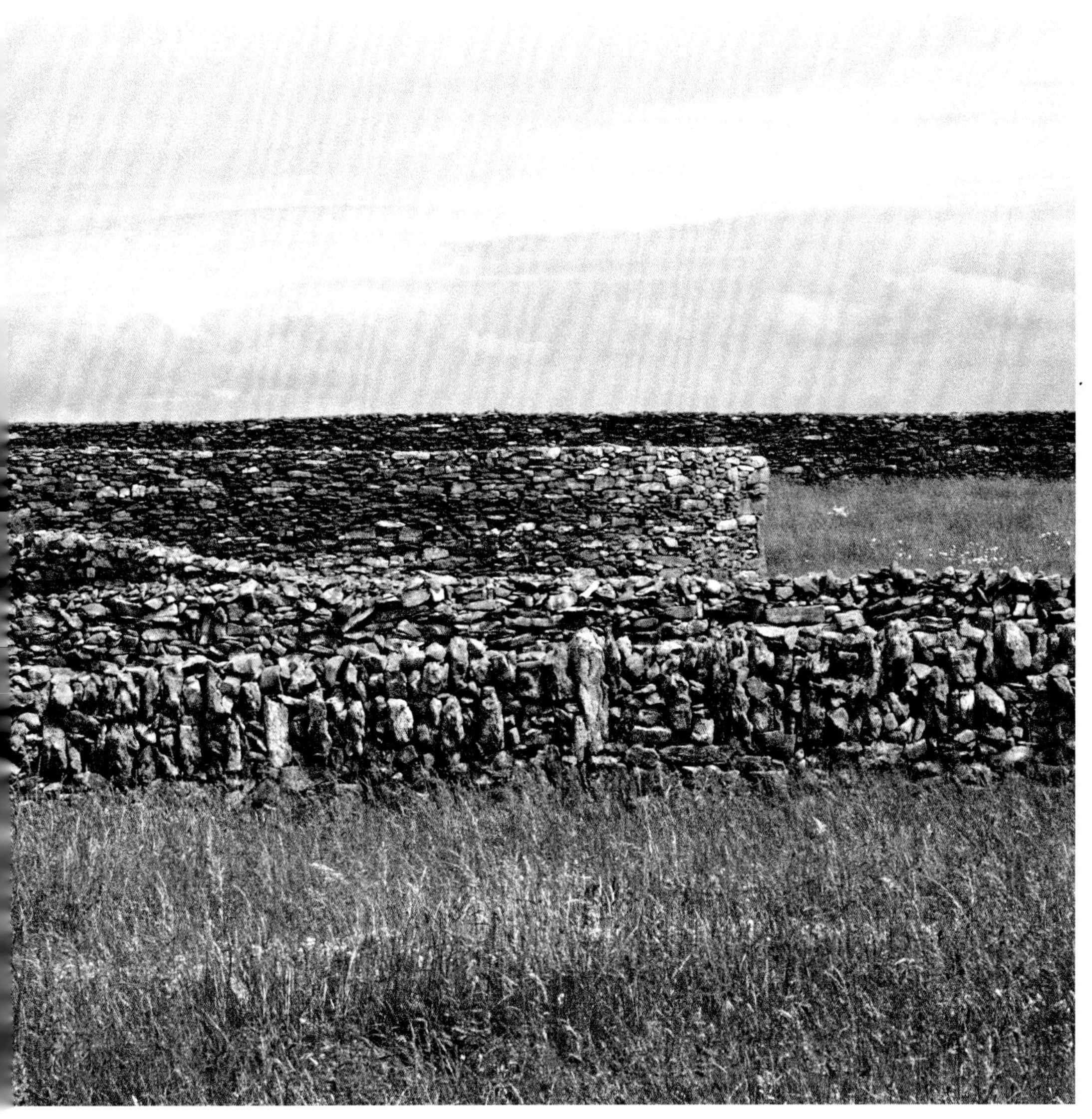

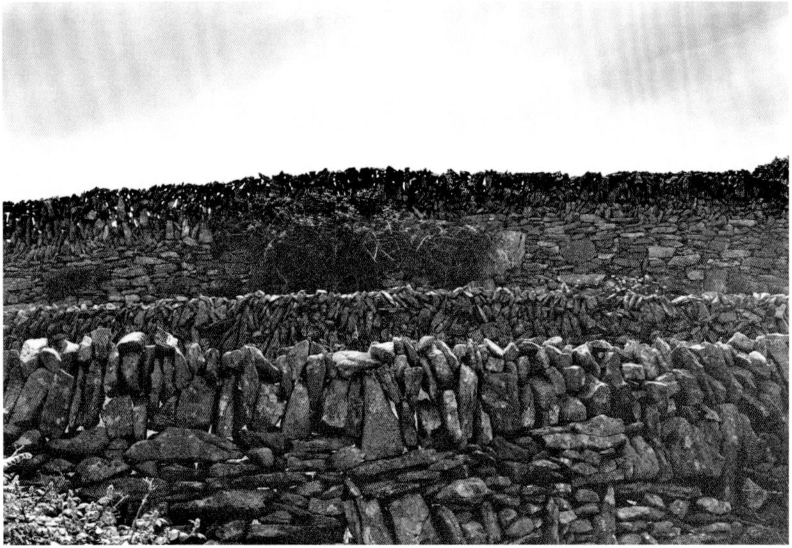

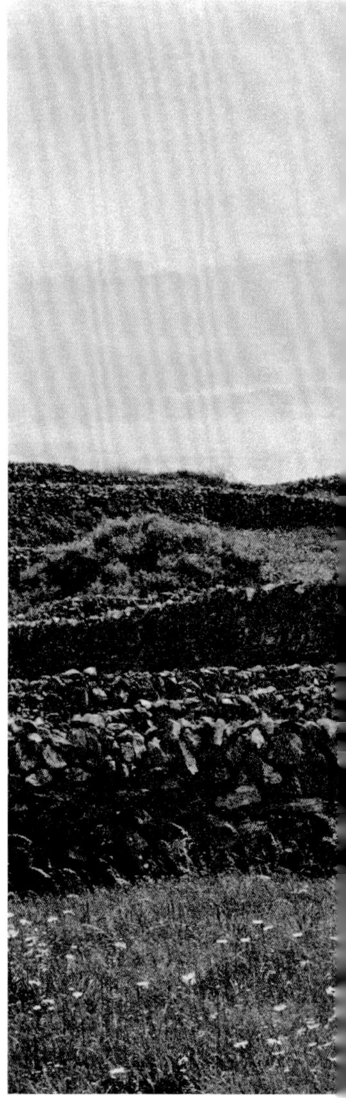

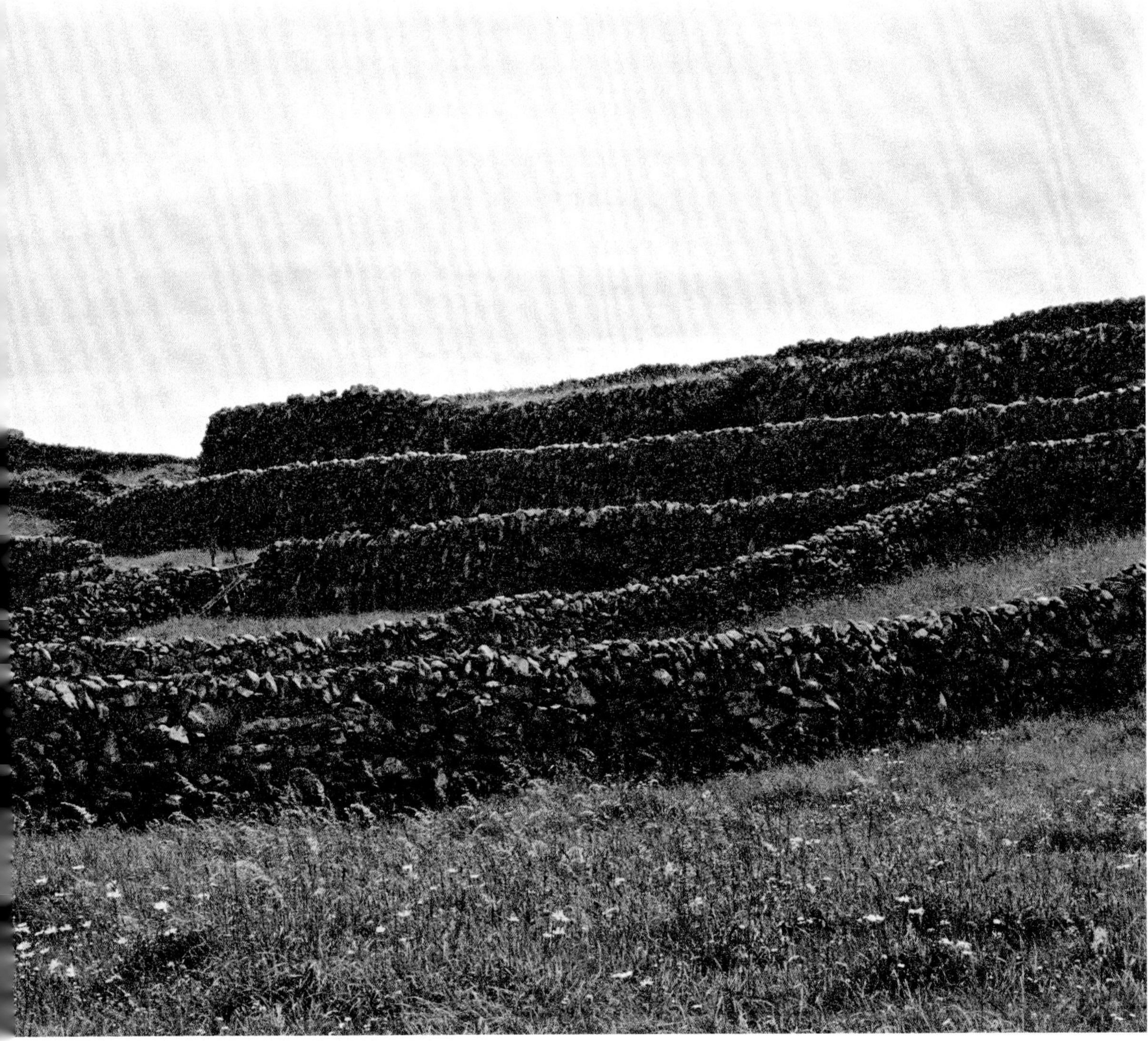

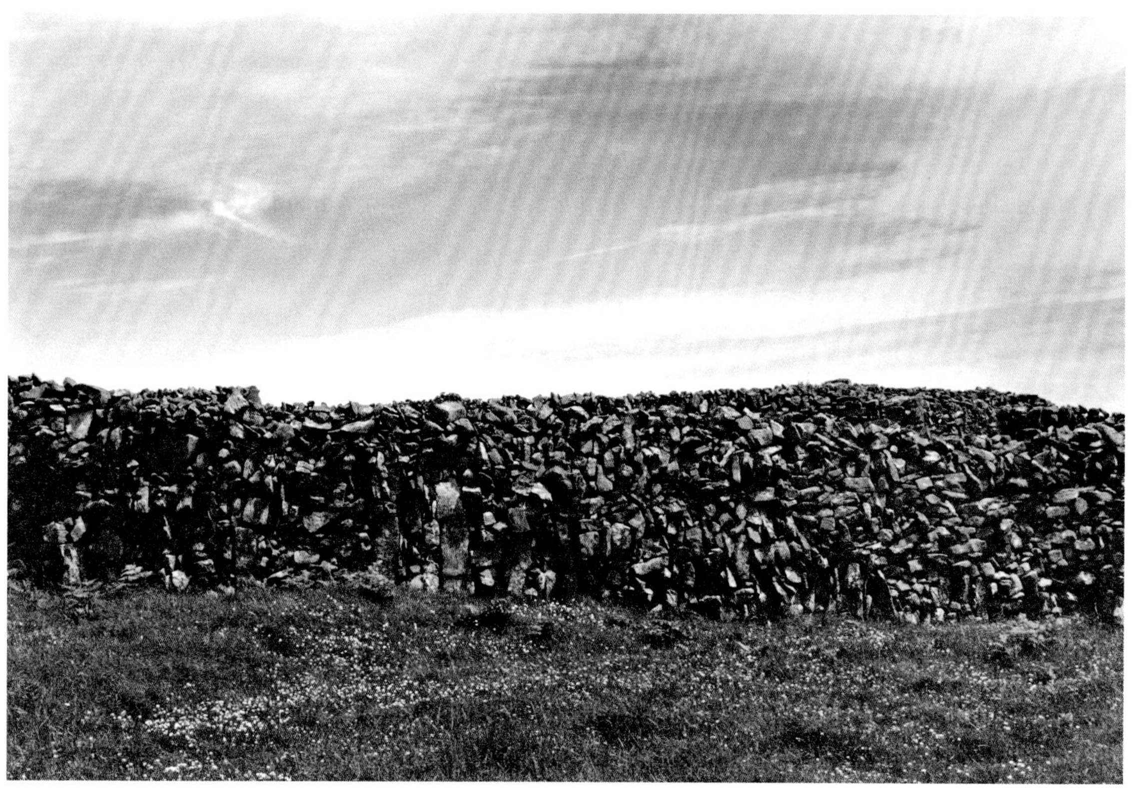

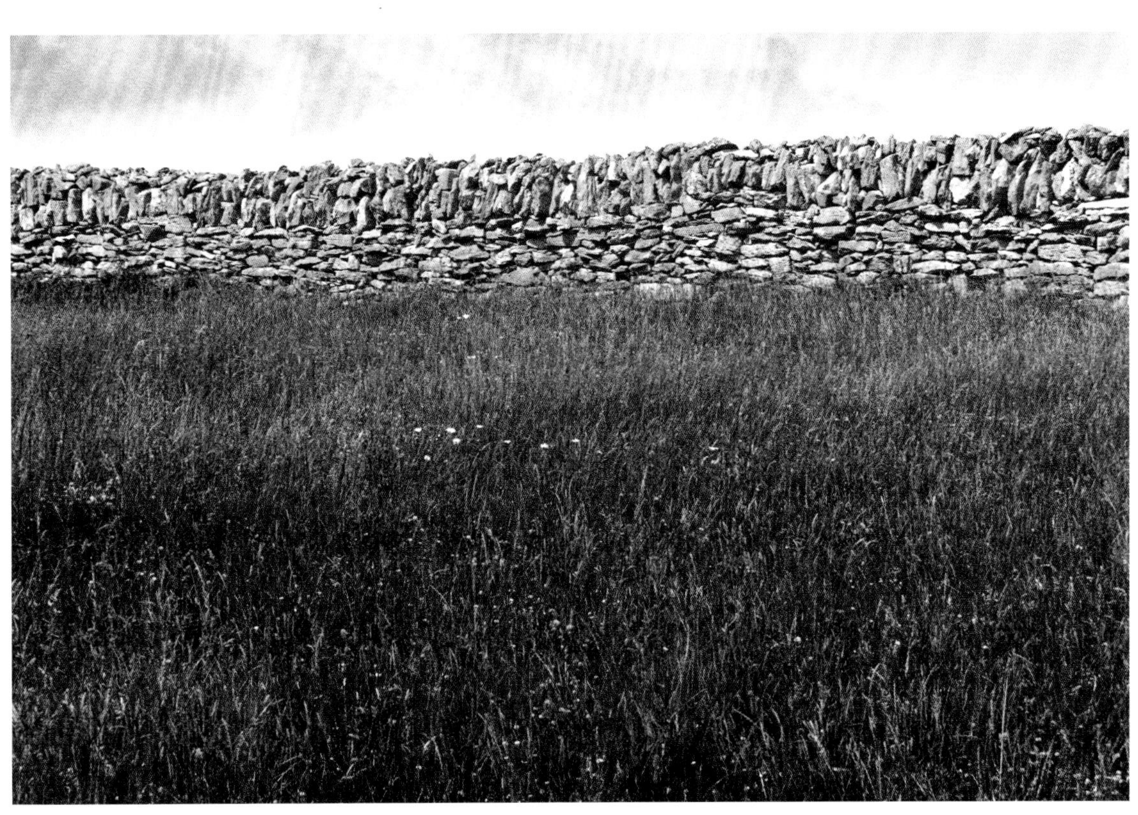

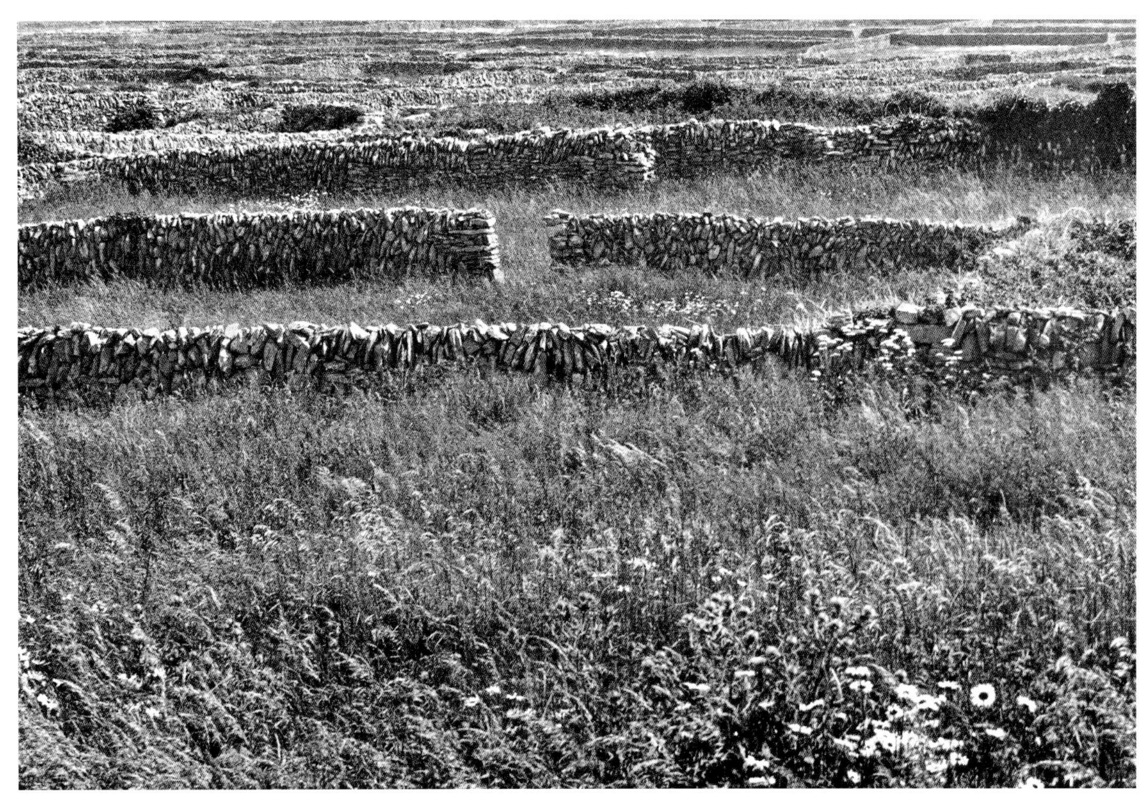

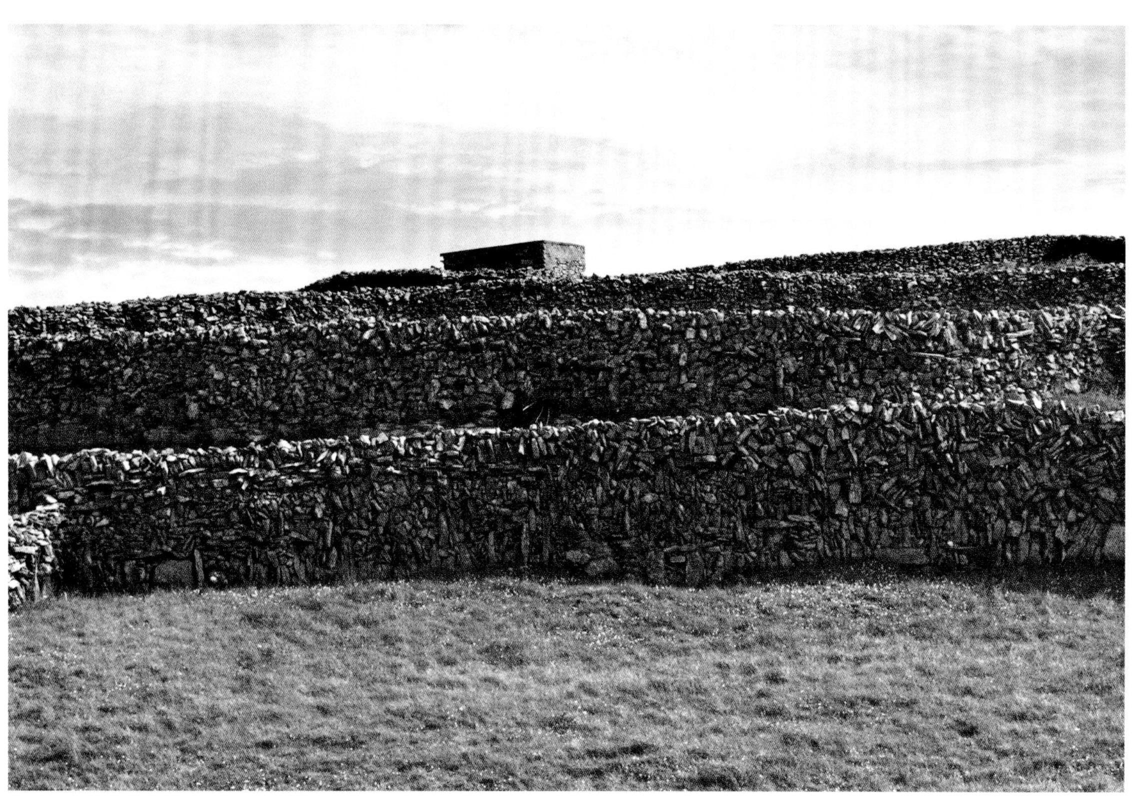

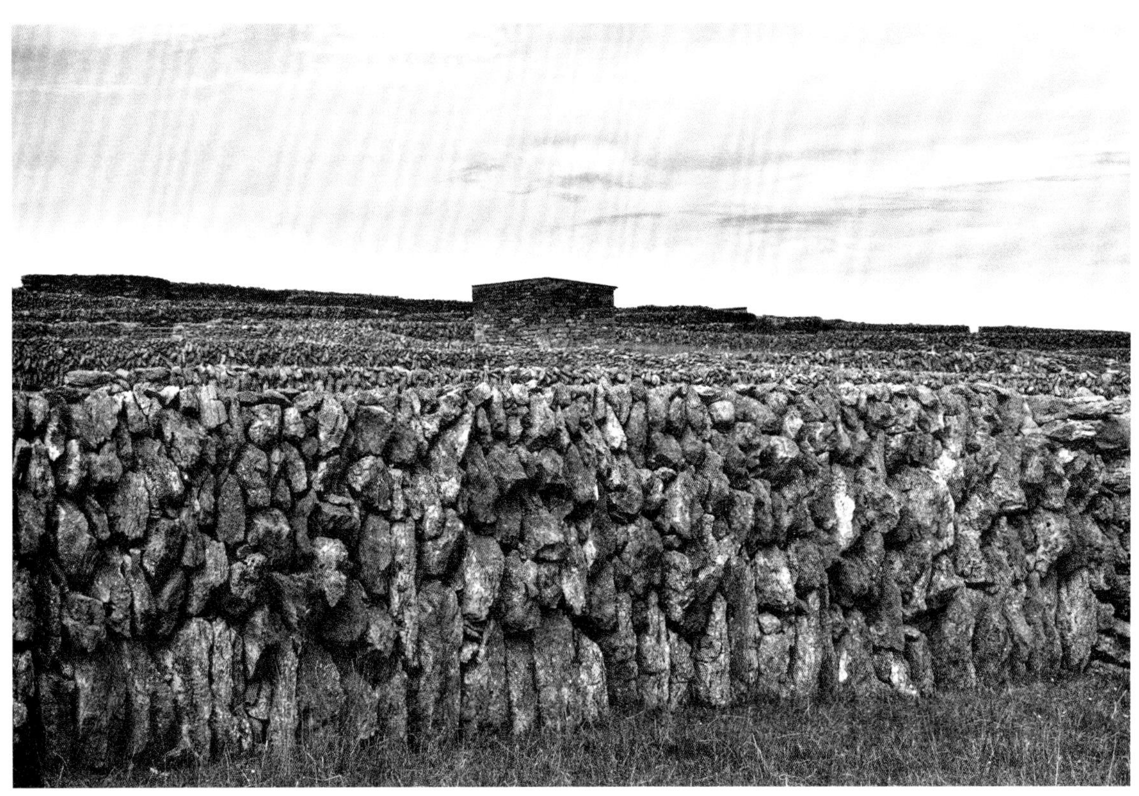

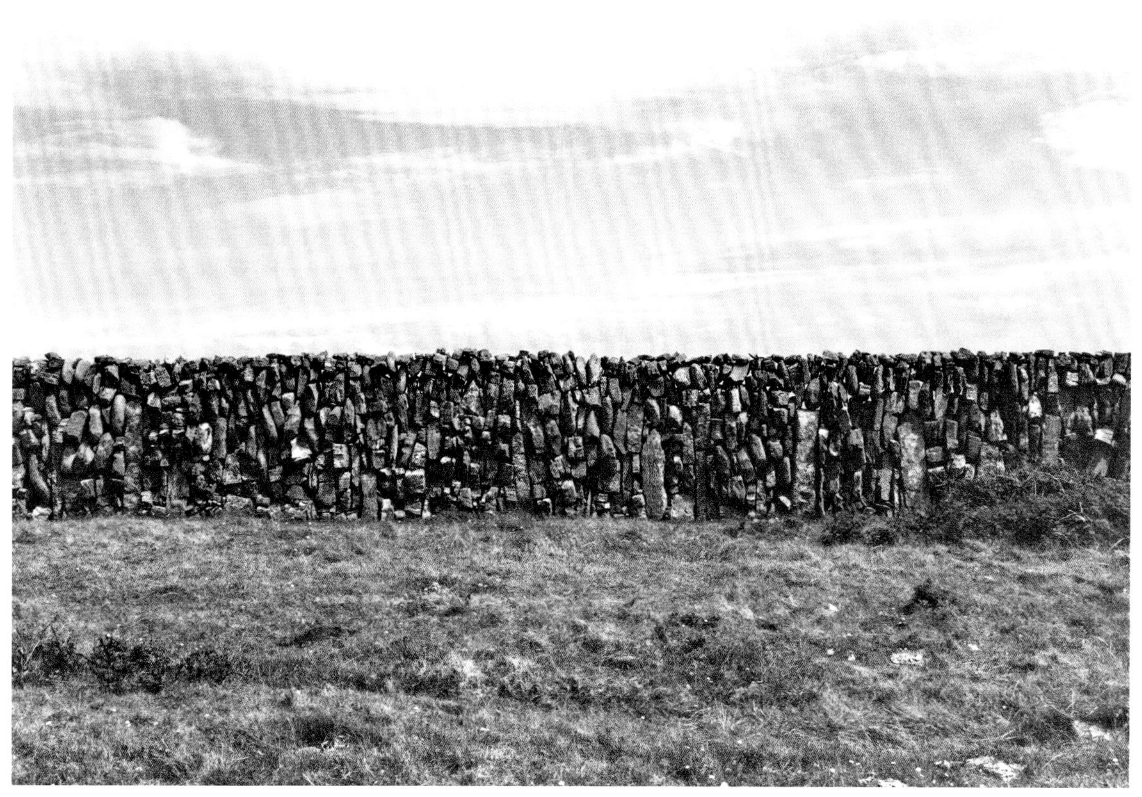

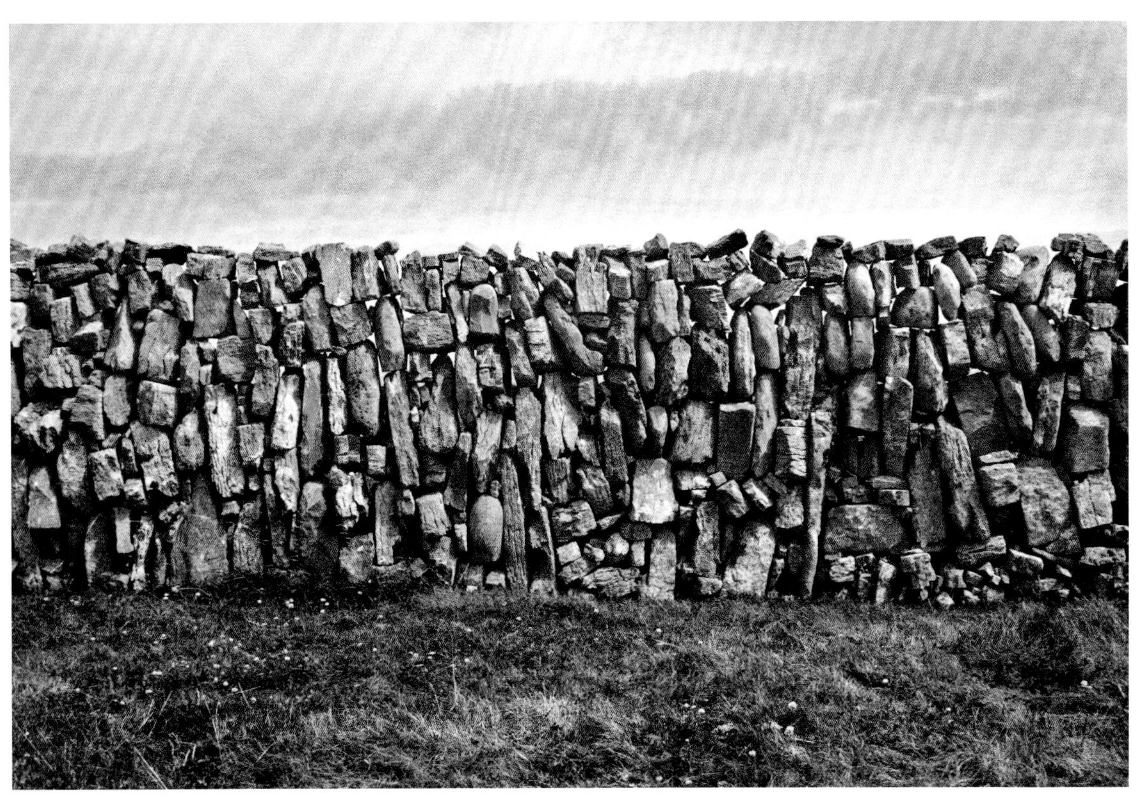

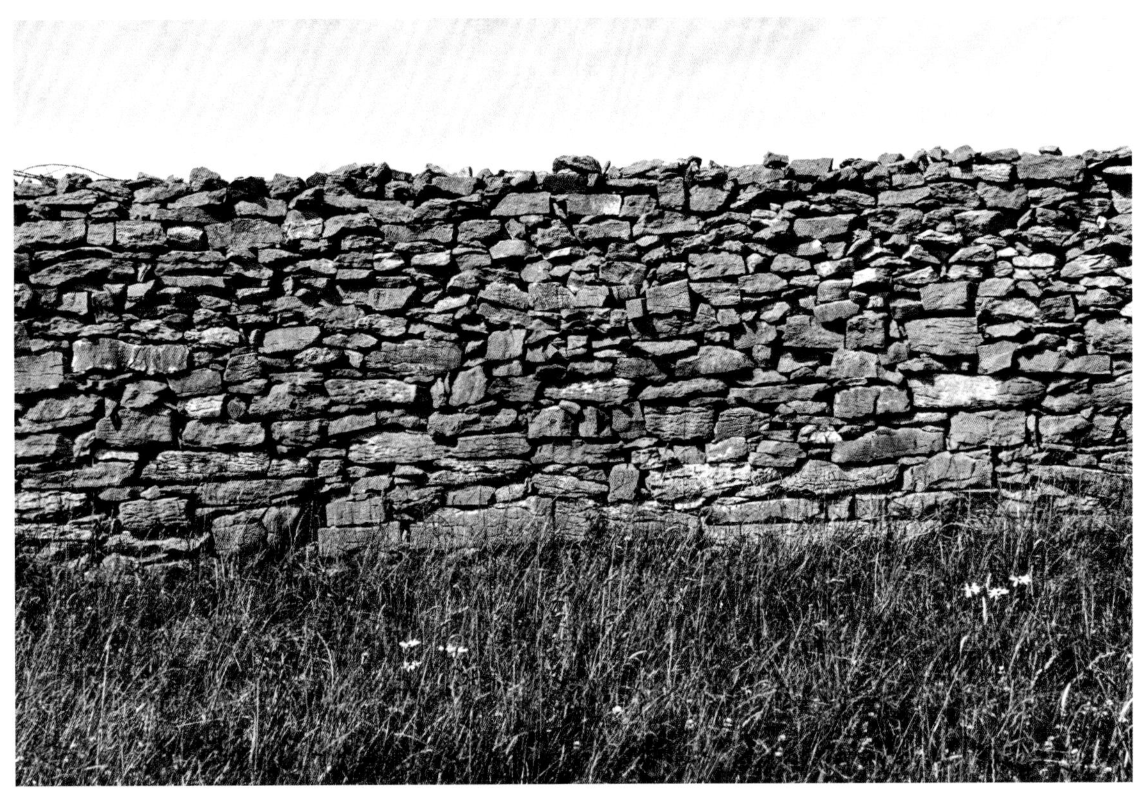

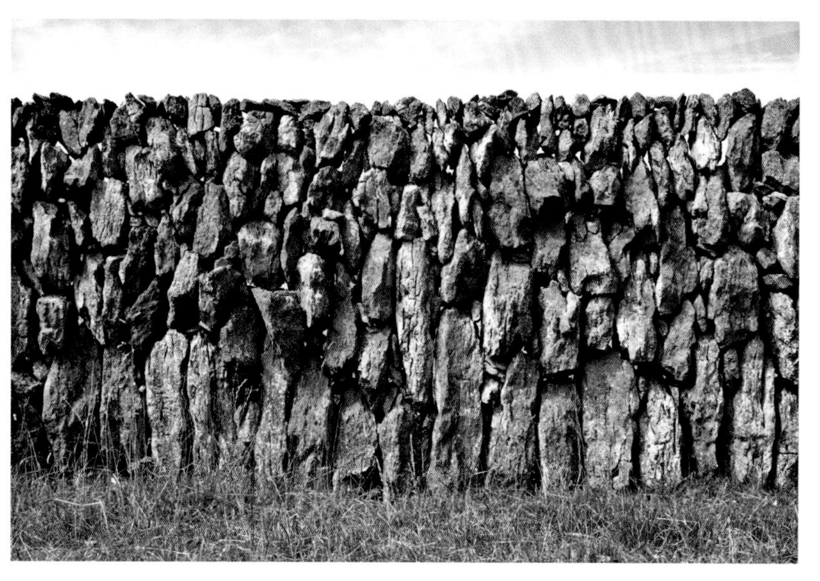
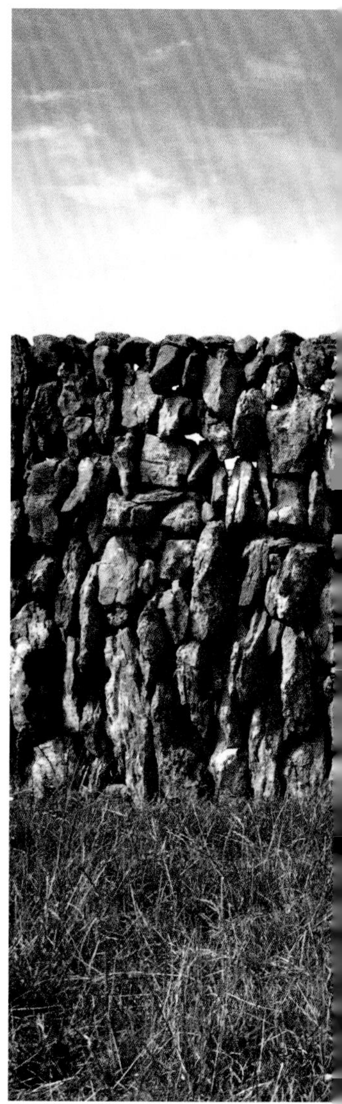

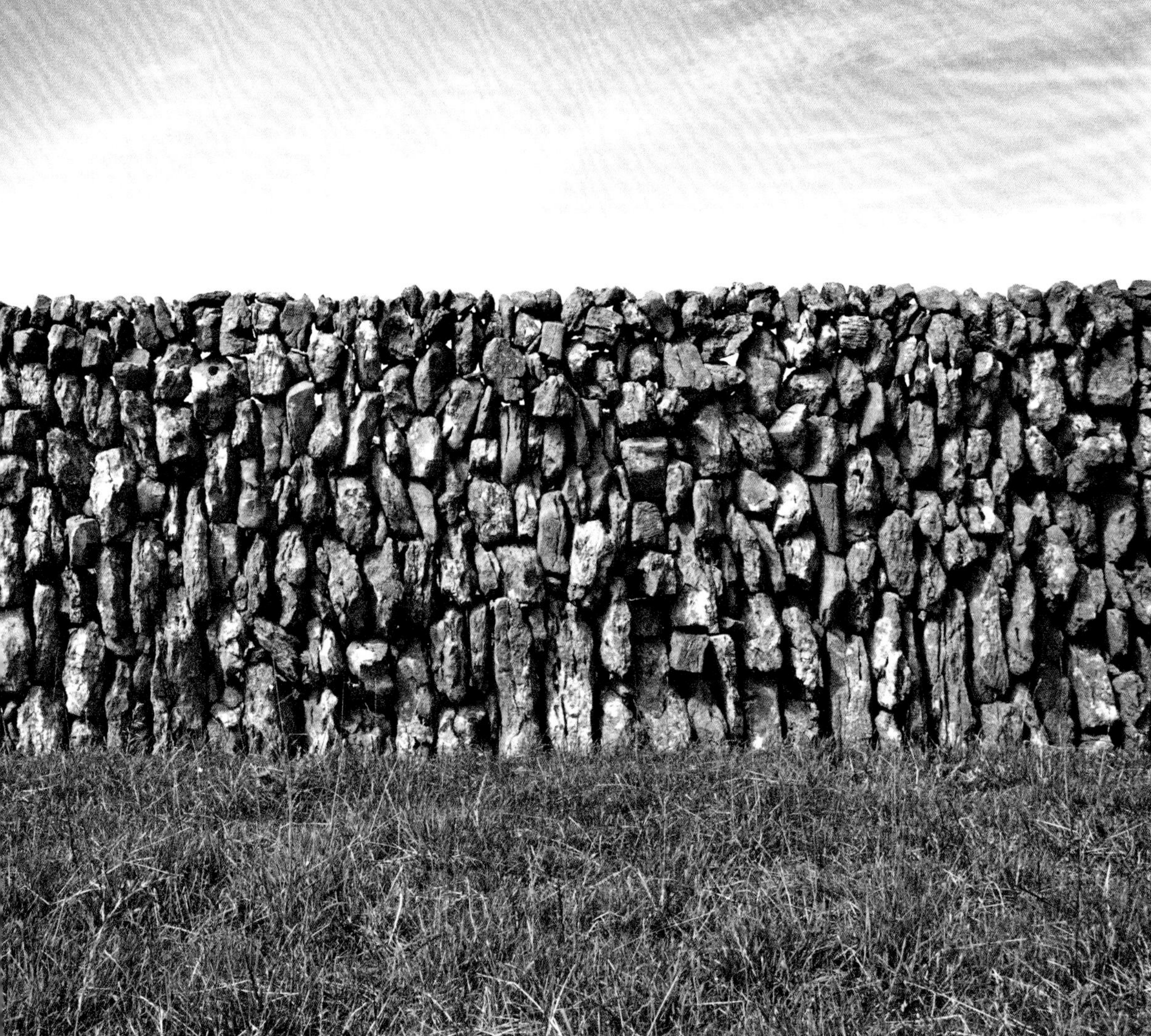

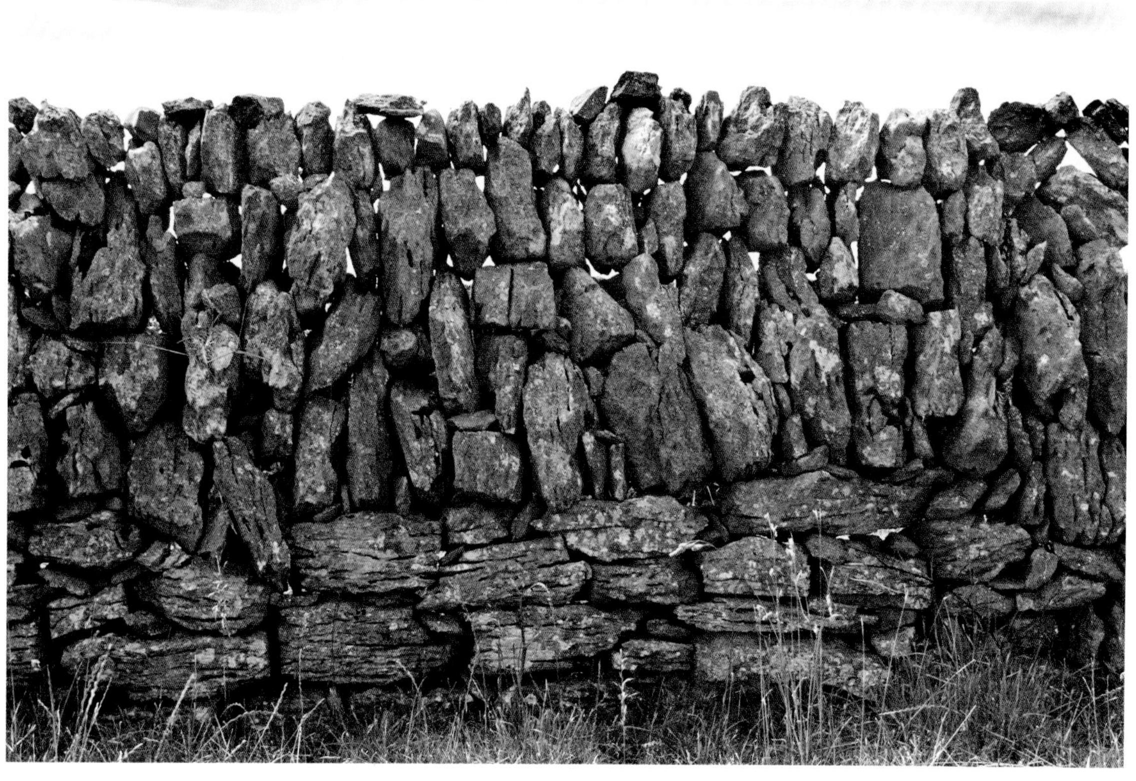

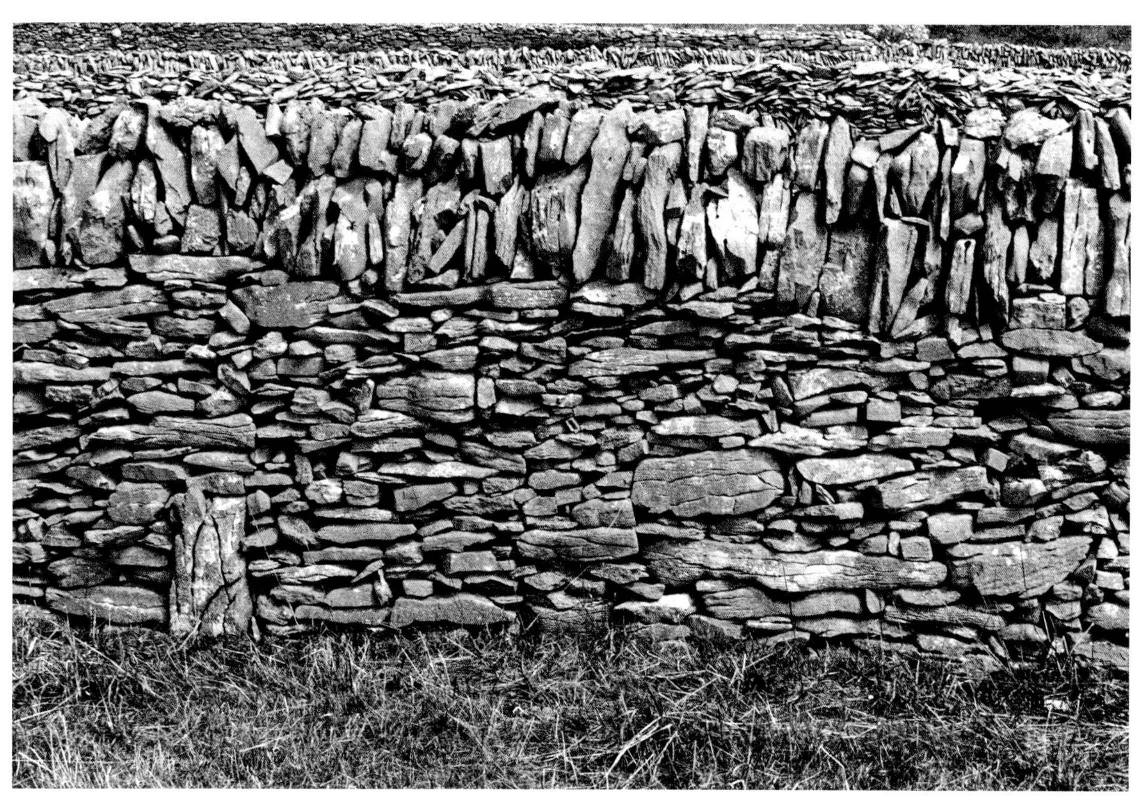

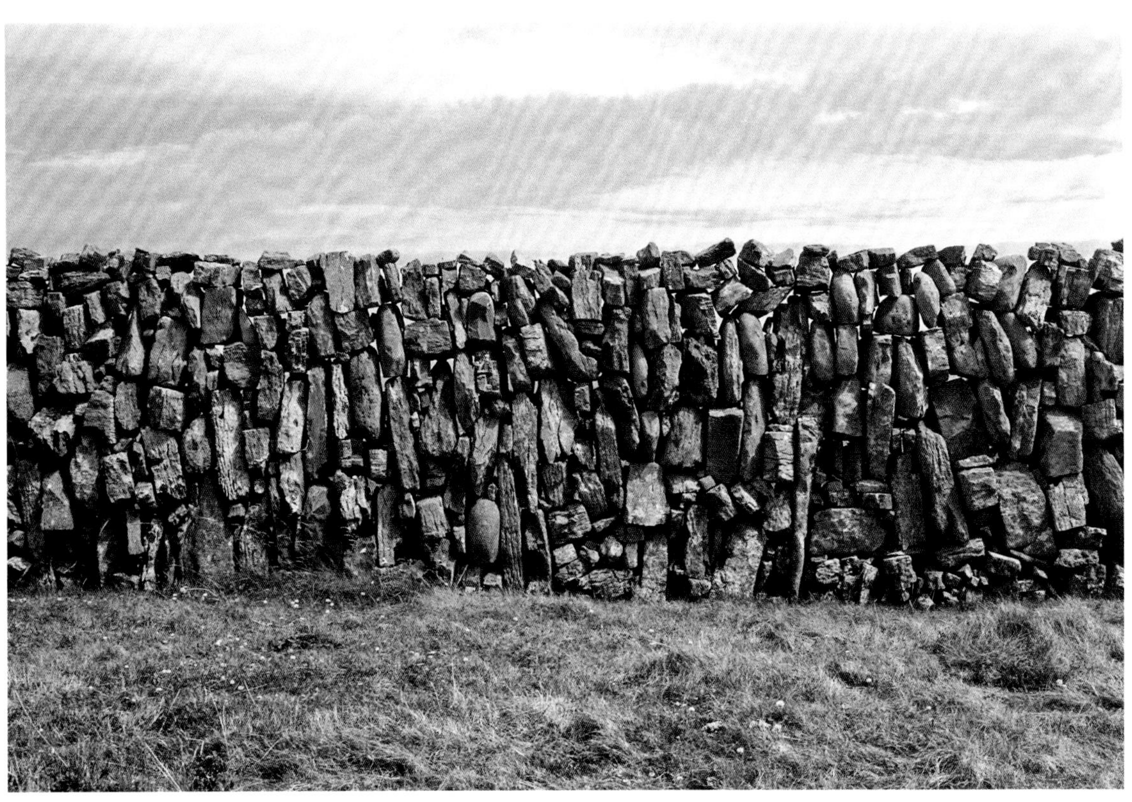

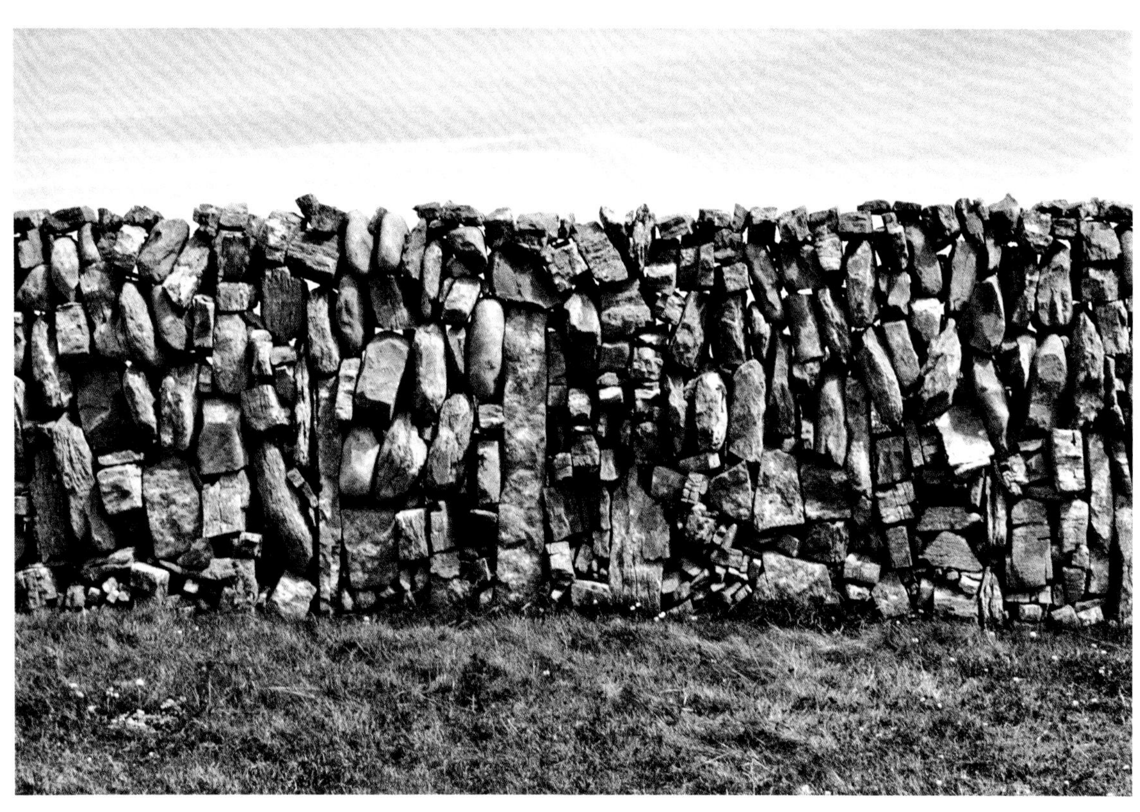

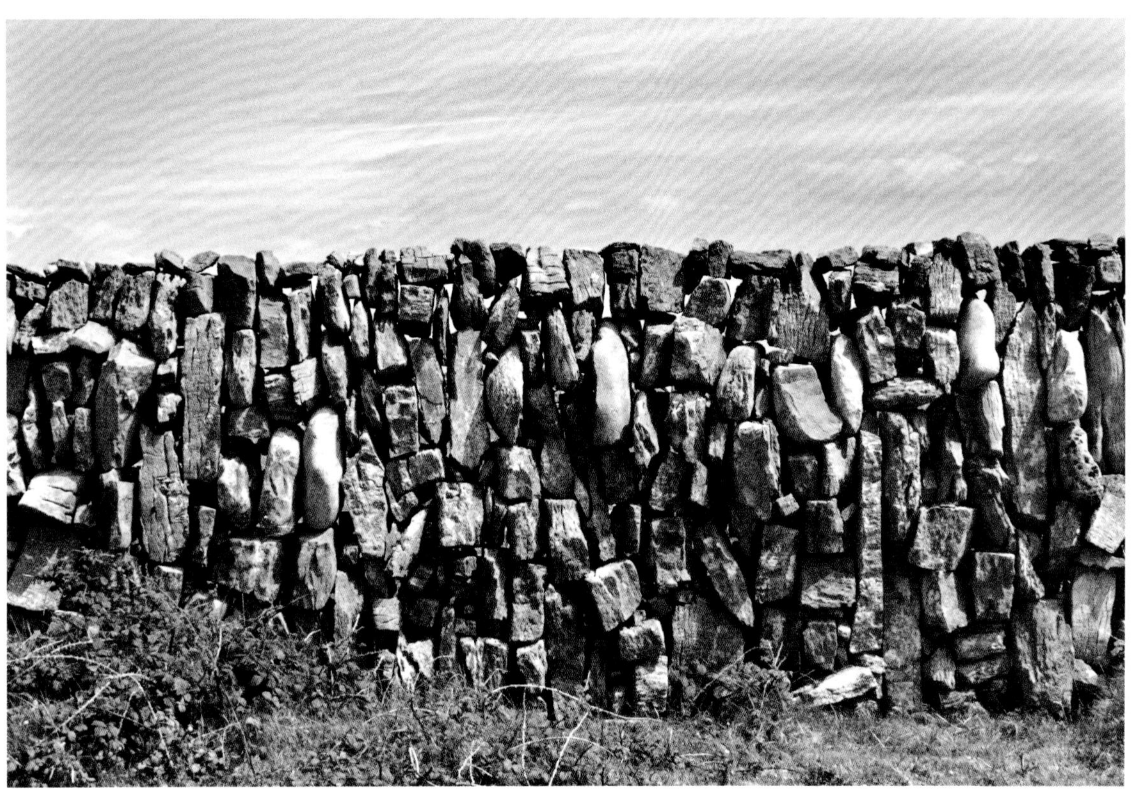

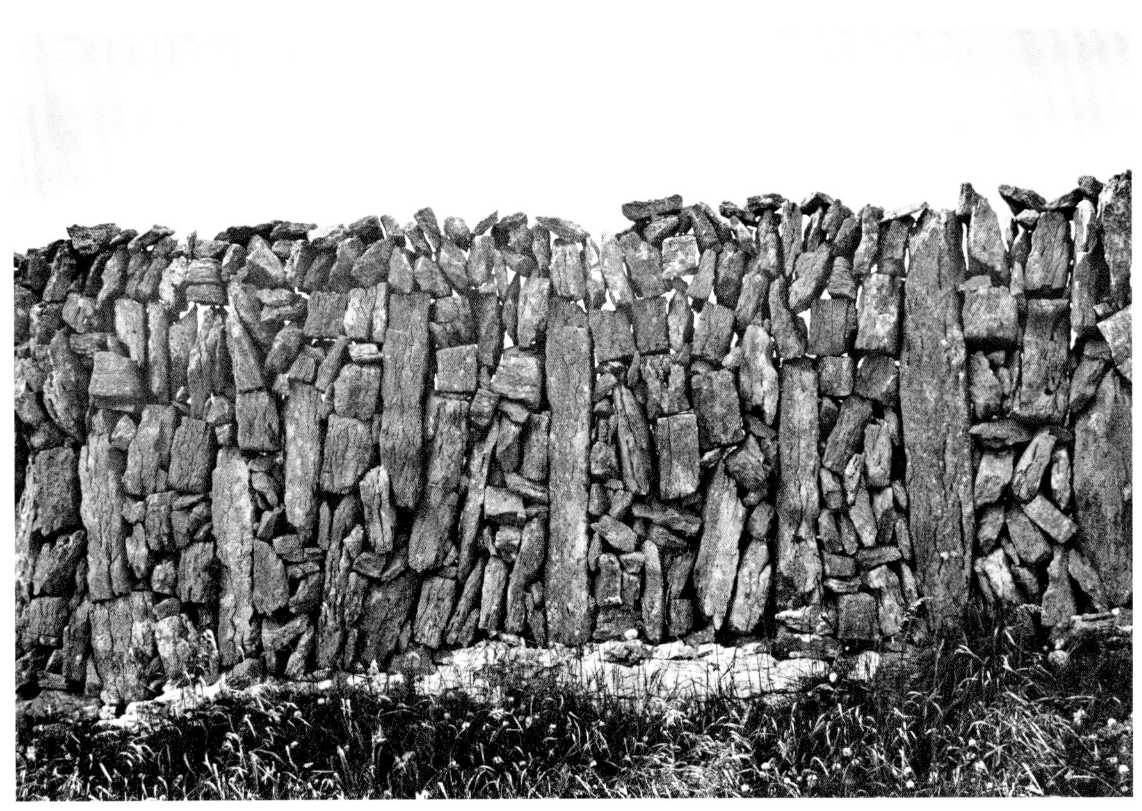

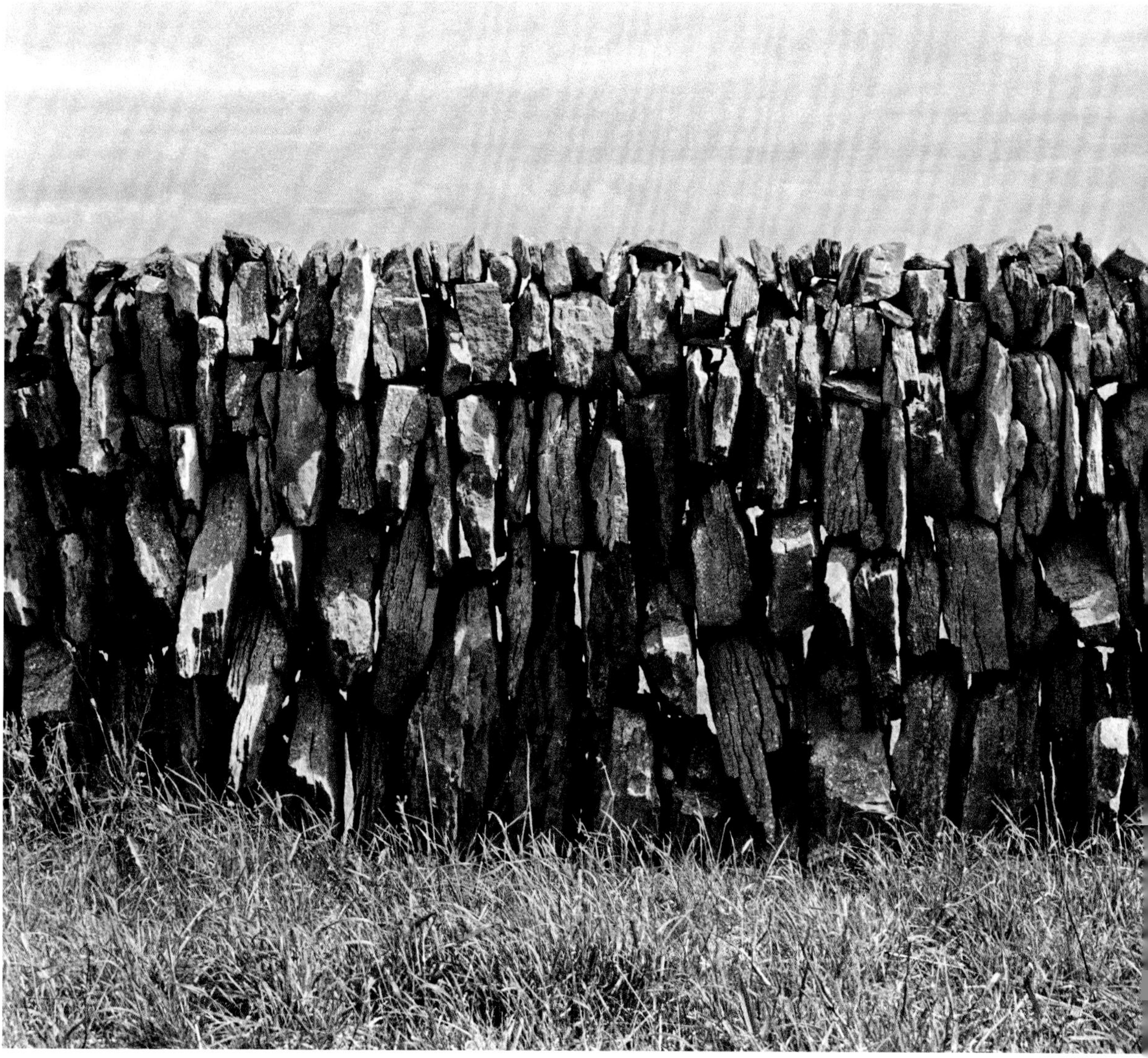

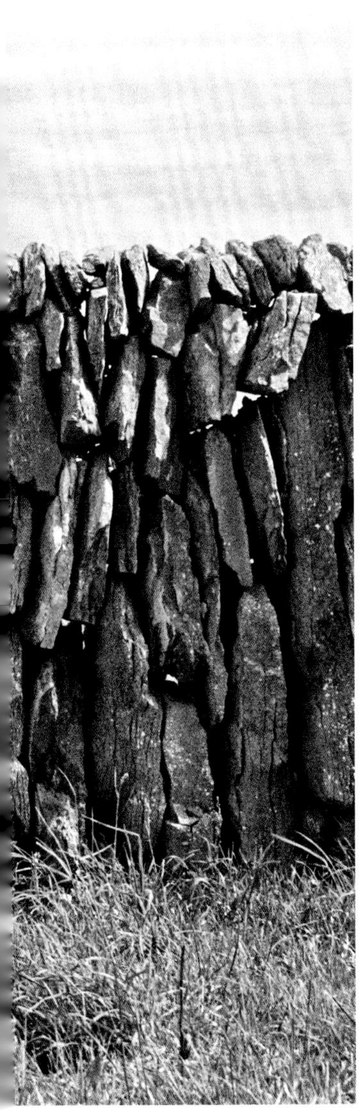

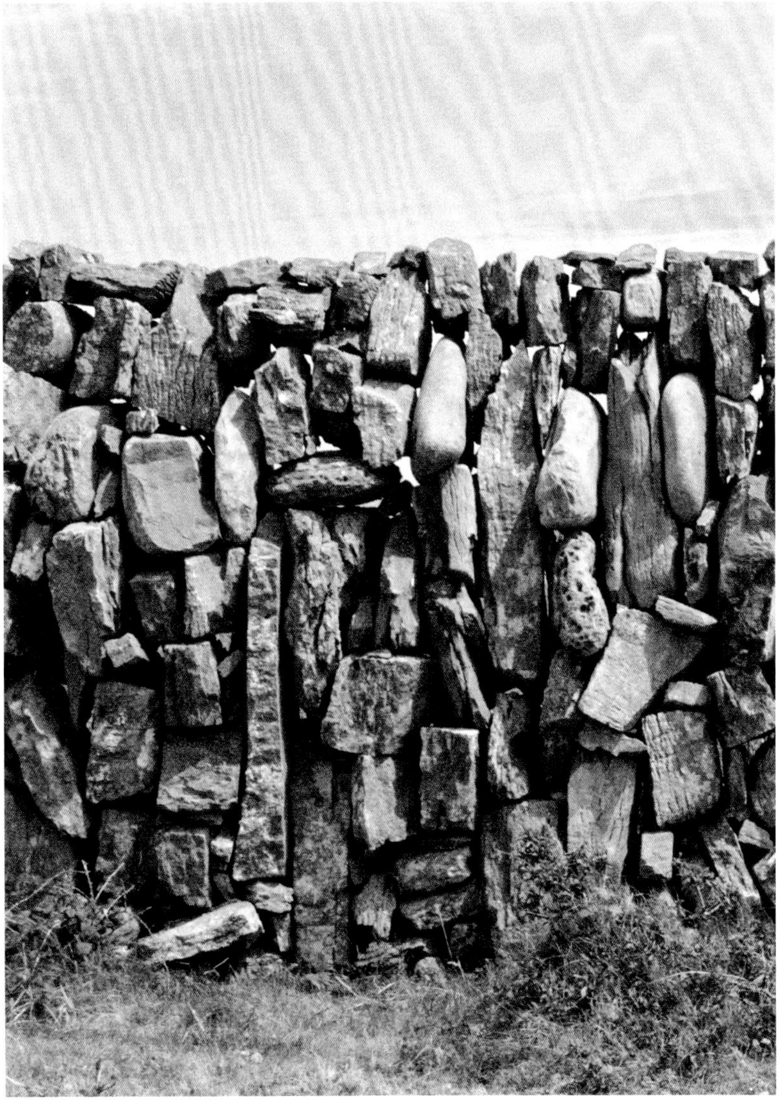

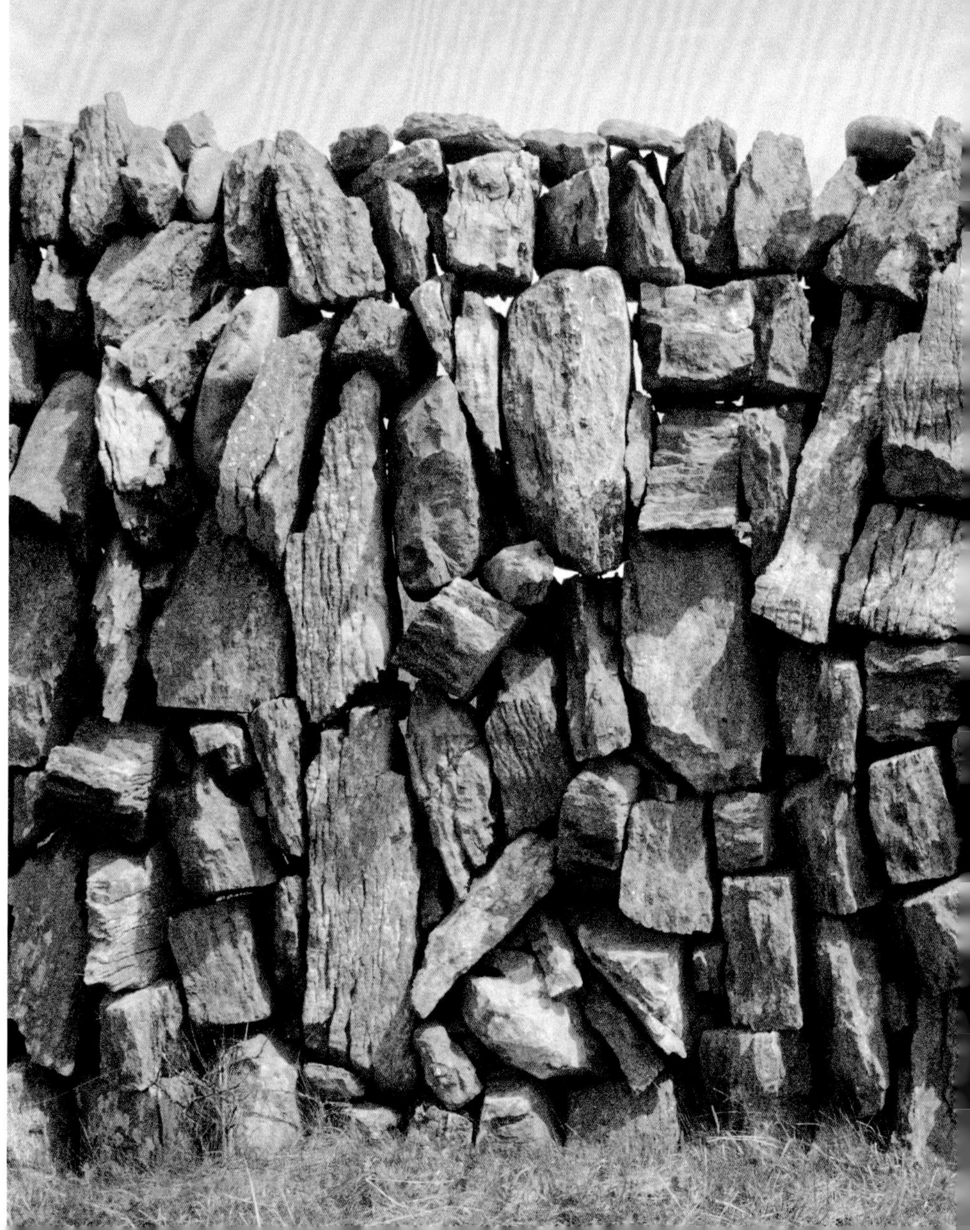

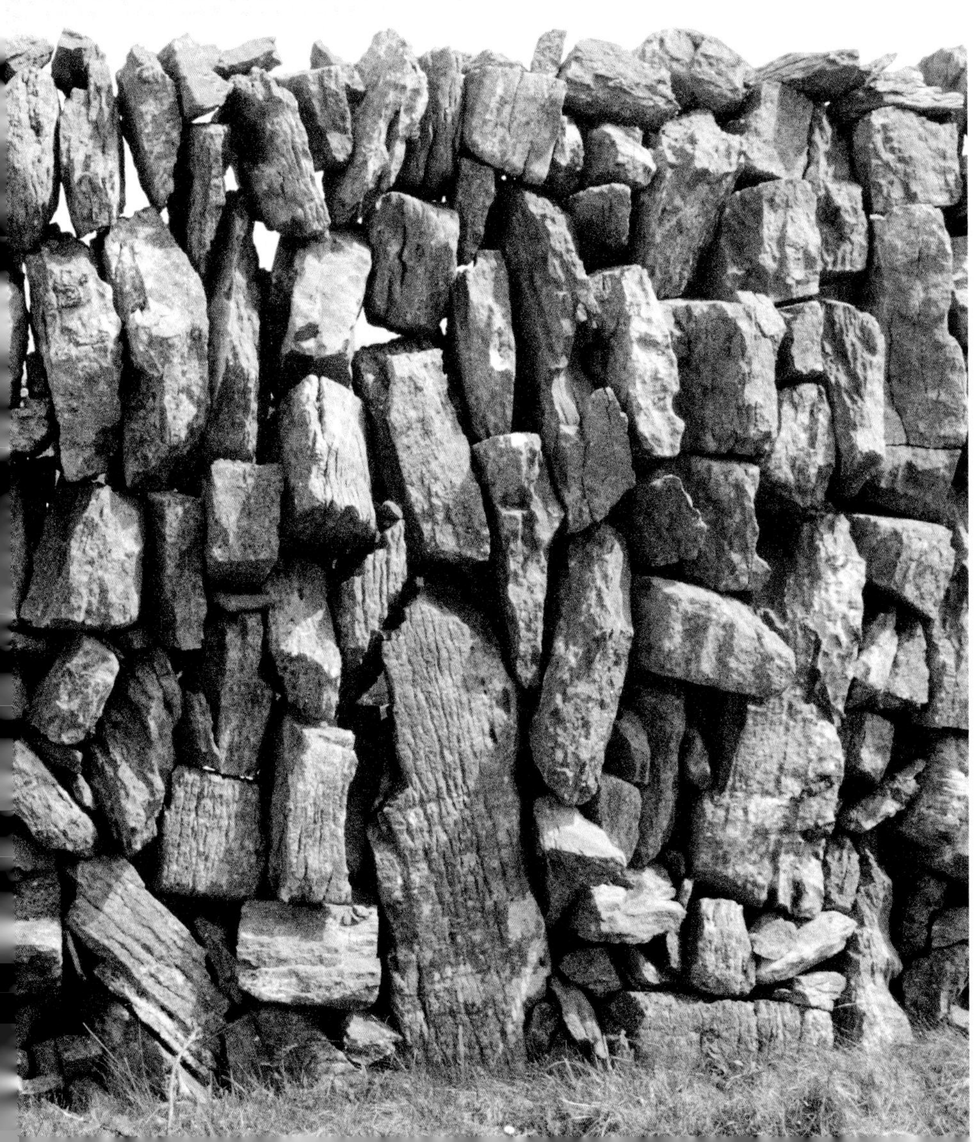

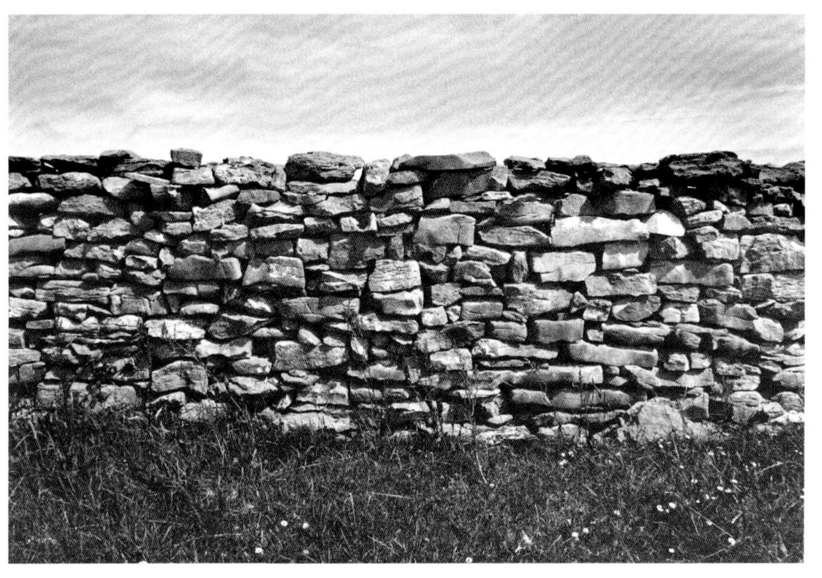

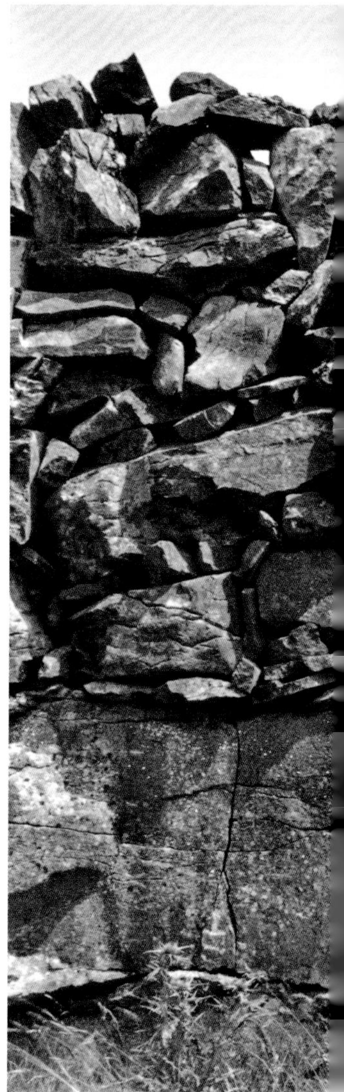

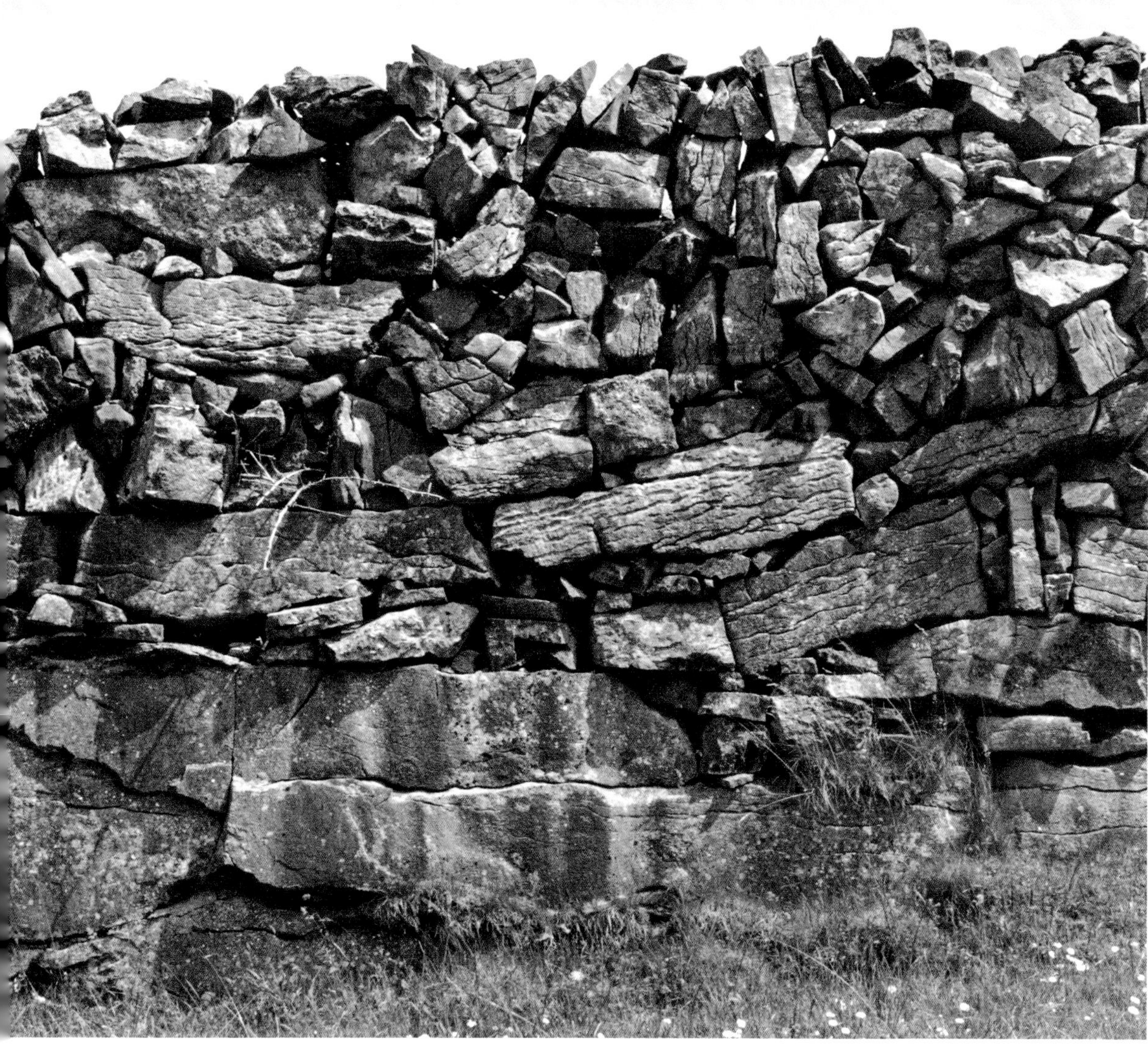

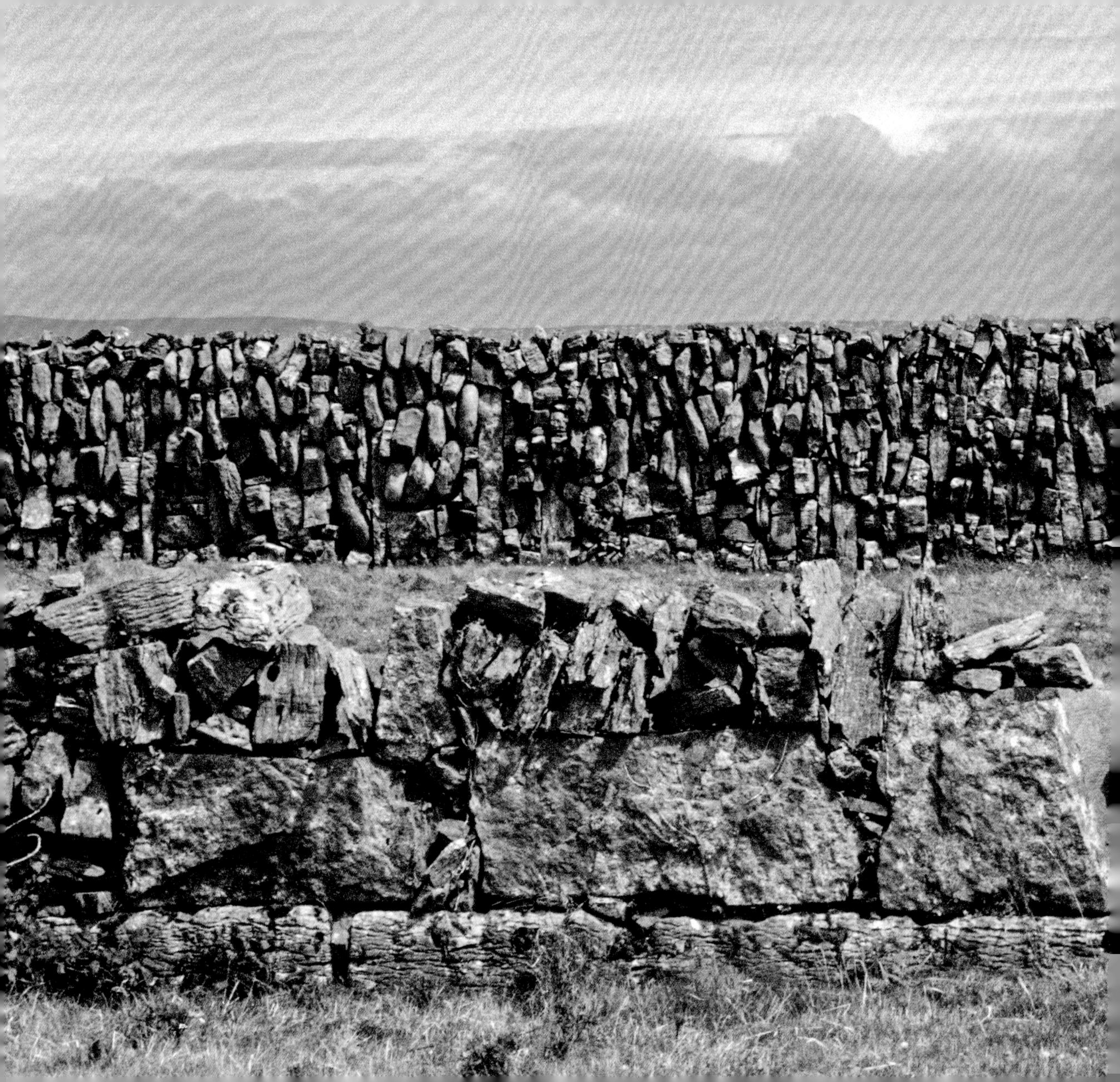

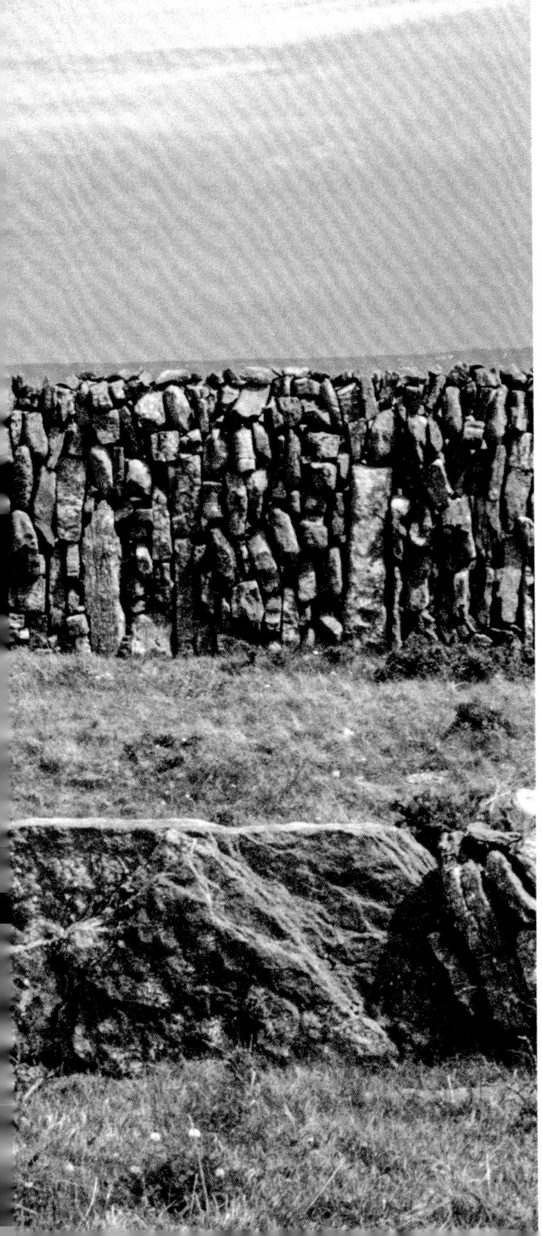

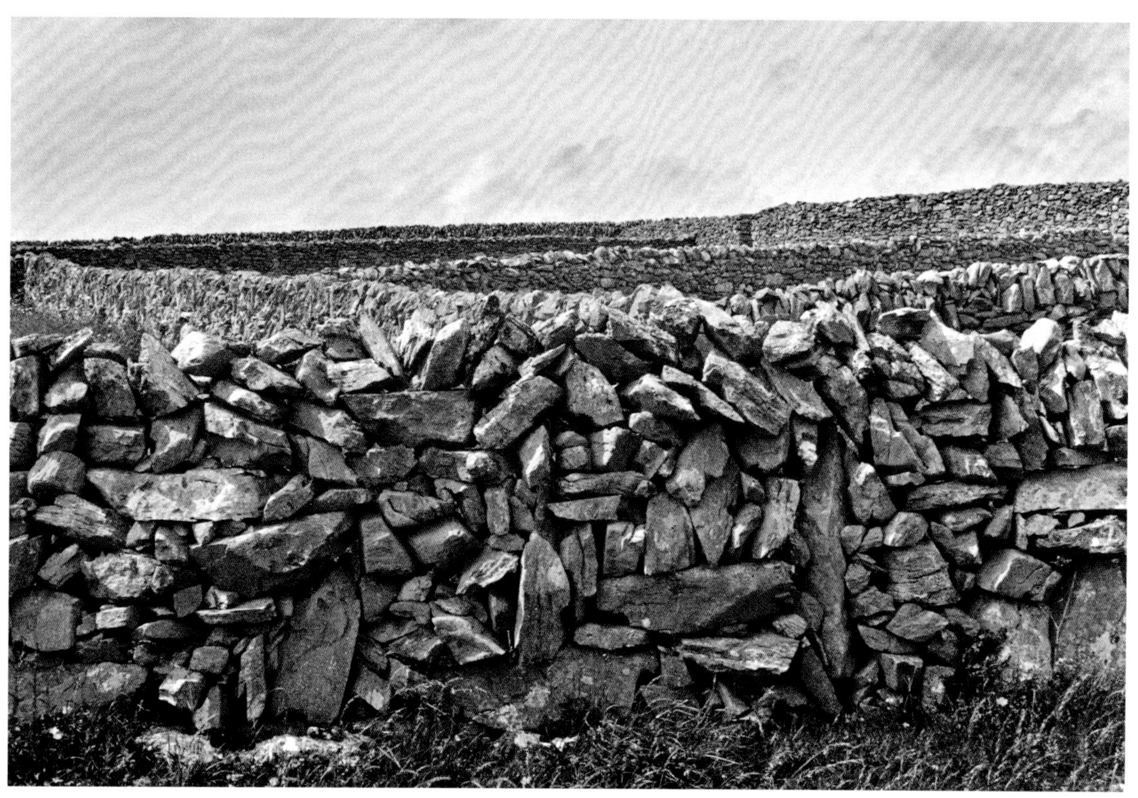

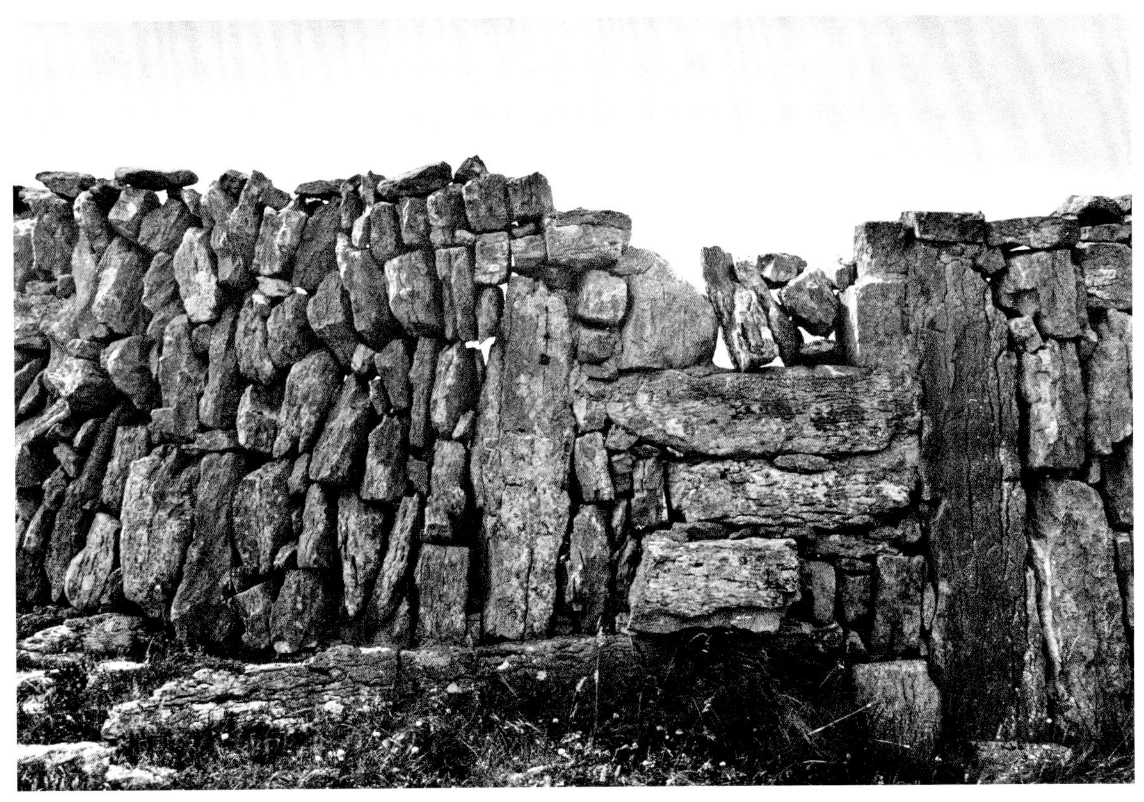

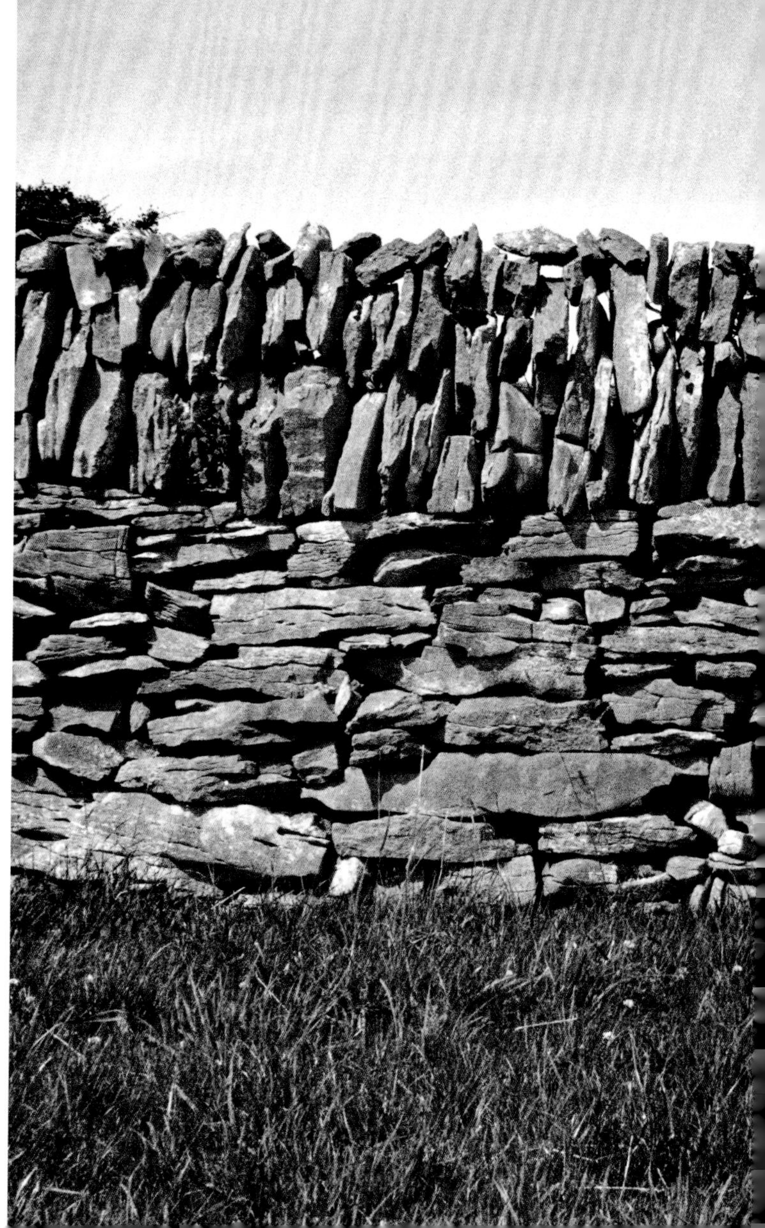

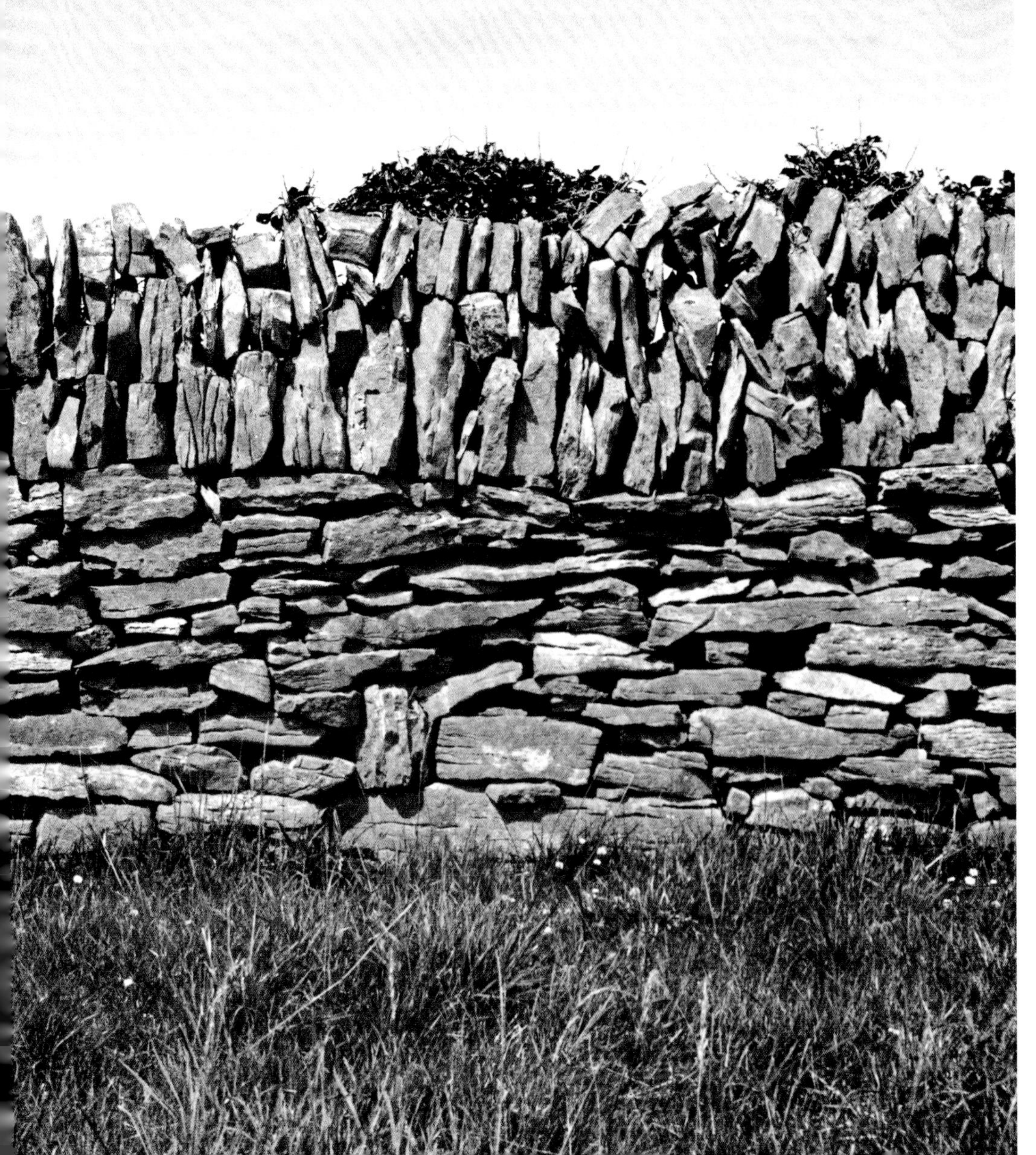

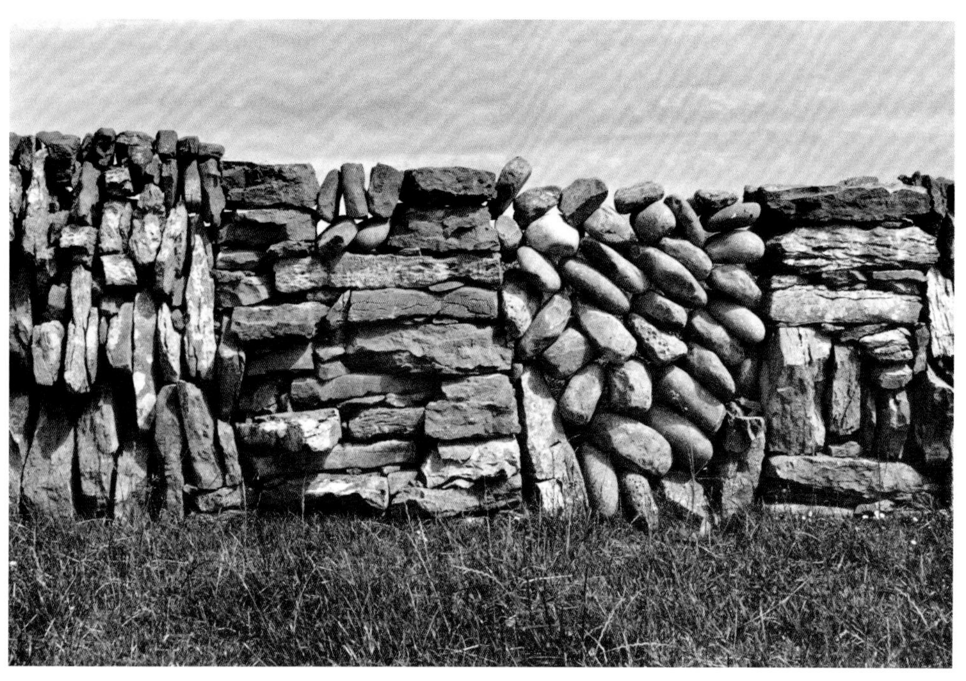

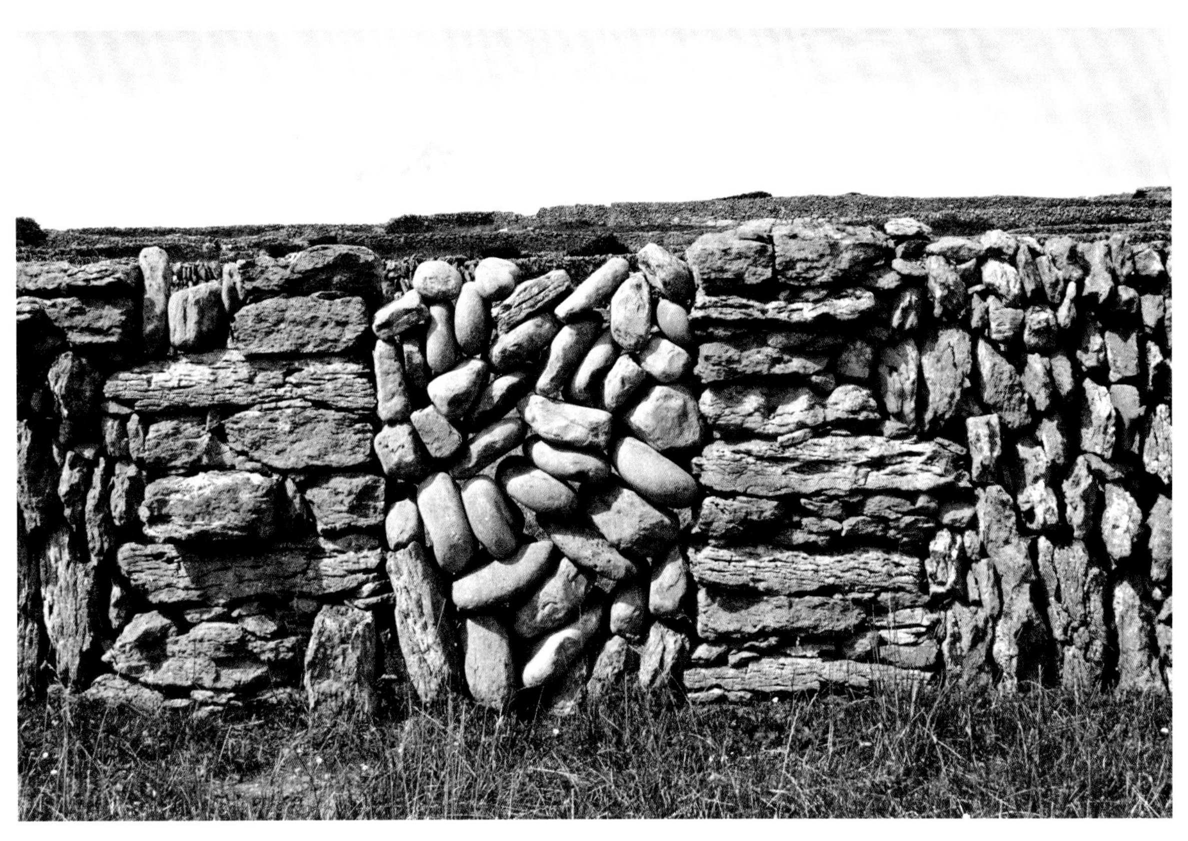

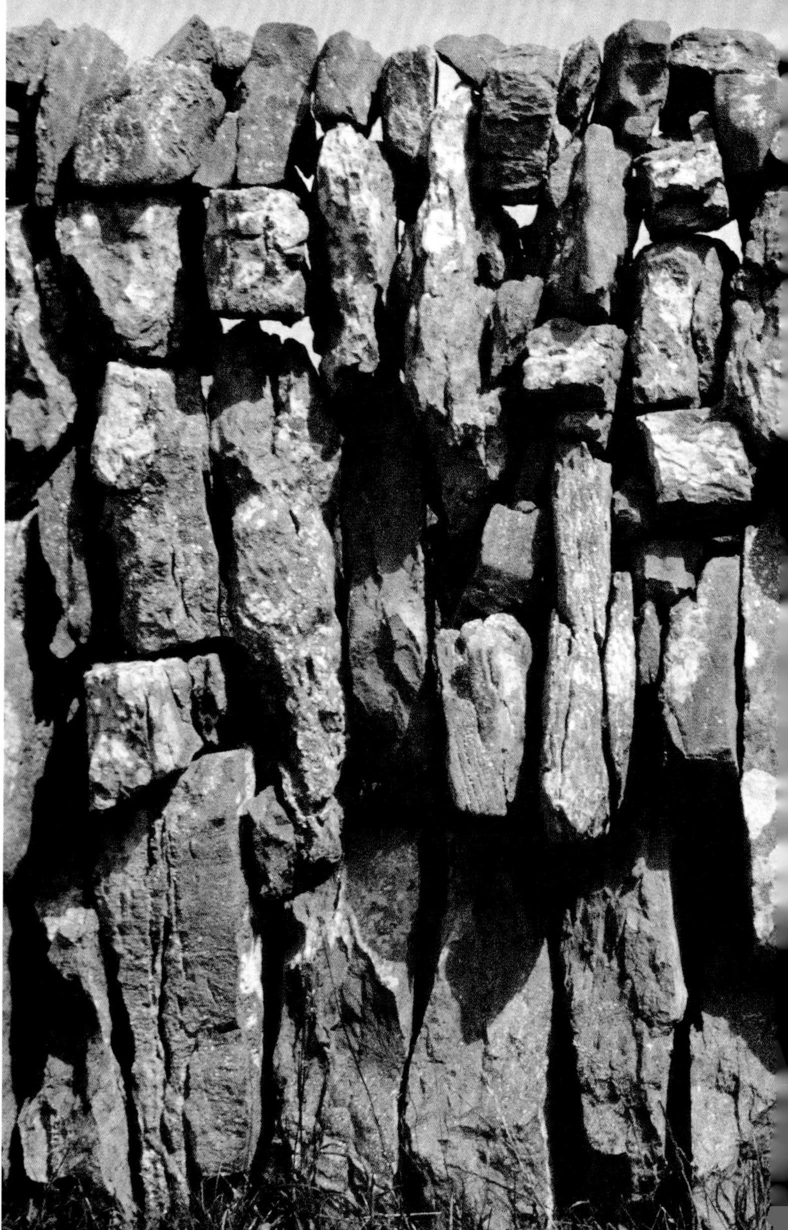

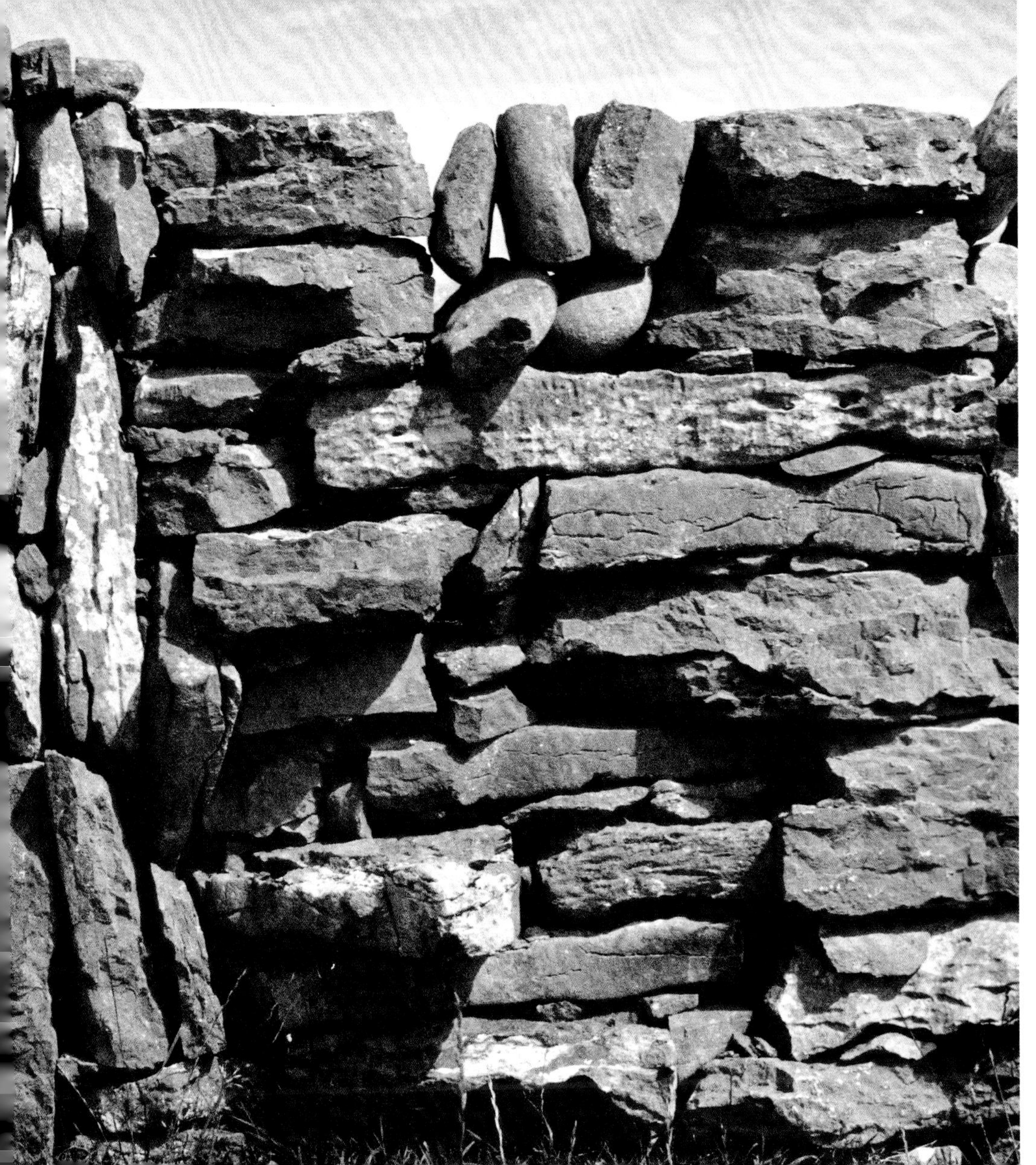

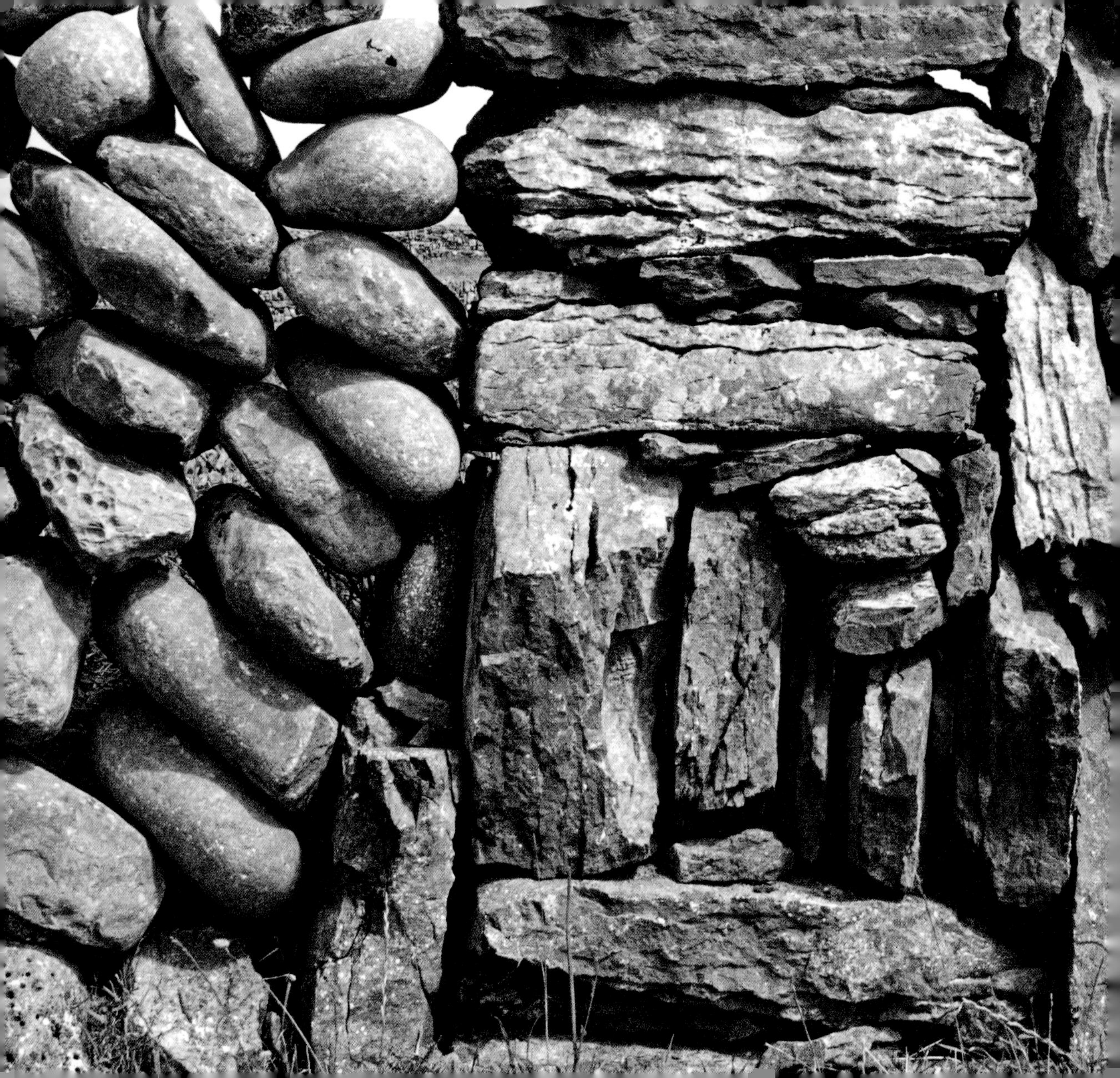

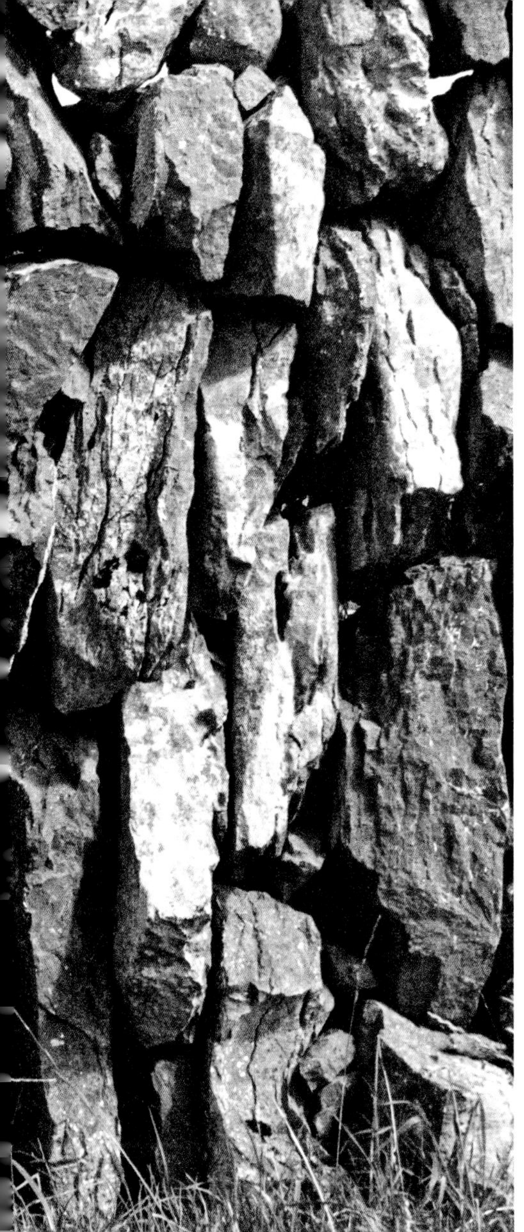

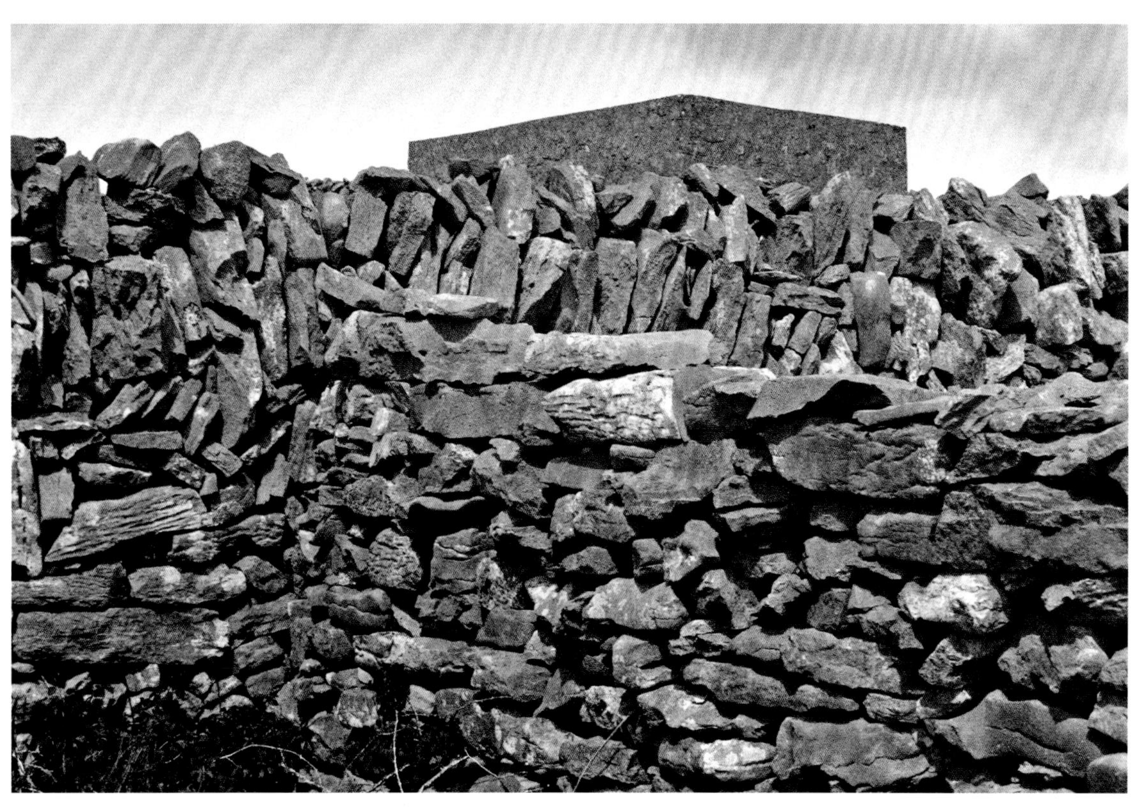

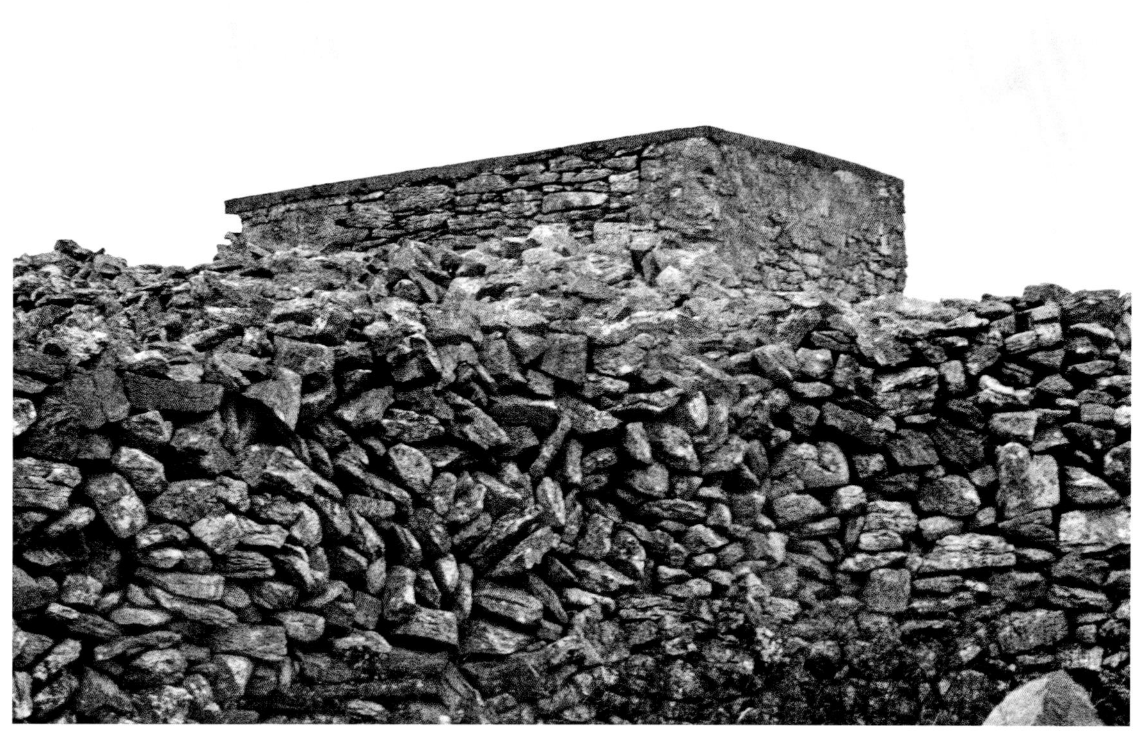

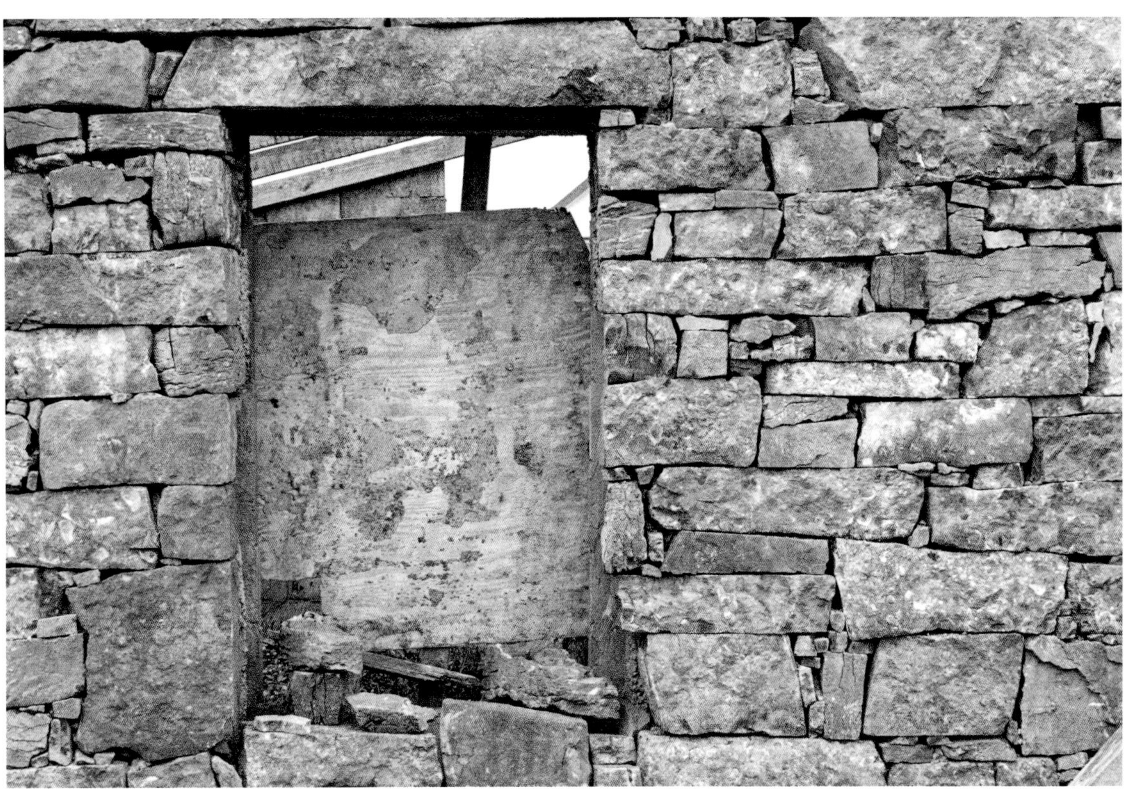

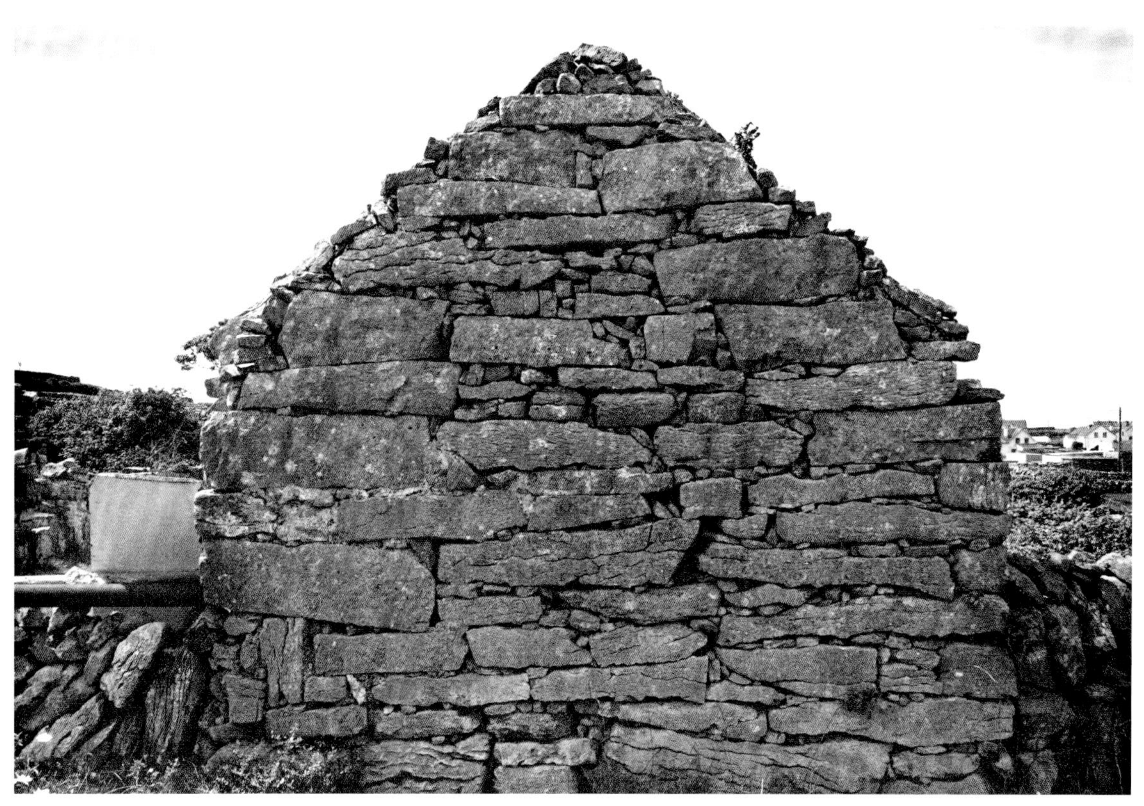

3

I cannot remember how I first came across Synge's play *Riders to the Sea*, but I think it was in the school library. Certainly, by the age of fifteen or sixteen, I had read it over and over and I knew some of the speeches off by heart. In my own fiction, three or four times as I was working on a novel or a story I was aware that I was drawing on the power and intensity of the play. But I had only seen it performed once – in an Irish-language version in a theatre in Dublin. Now, in 2005, I learned that the Druid Theatre Company in Galway was going to perform it on Inis Meáin as part of a cycle of all Synge's plays, directed by Garry Hynes, whose work I admired. They were going to do the plays in Dún Chonchúir which was the most impressive fort or cashel on the Aran Islands after Dún Aonghasa on Árainn, the largest island. (Its main wall forms an oval more than two hundred feet long and more than a hundred feet broad, with walls and terraces nineteen feet in thickness. It looks like a theatre.)

I also learned that they were going to do *Riders to the Sea* for the people of the island, rather than visitors who might travel to see the cycle, earlier in the week.

I thought I would break the spell and go to Inis Meáin for the first time to see the play with the great Irish actress Marie Mullen playing Maurya on the very island which had given Synge his inspiration in the presence of the people who still inhabited the elements in which the drama unfolded.

I flew over on a calm day in early September and found a place to stay. As soon as I arrived I walked out without a map, following my nose, wandering down to the pier first, as Synge must have done so often, to see if there was anything happening there and then to the south, keeping to the edge of the coast as much as I could, so that I had a clear view of Inis Oírr. I saw no one on that walk, or on any other of the walks I took on Inis Meáin. The thousands of day trippers who arrived every day on Árainn did not come here; the campers who came to Inis Oírr avoided Inis Meáin. It still remained, despite the improved access, the hidden and unvisited island.

I was amazed sometimes in Synge's book at finding that he had fallen asleep in the open air on the island. I walked along a surface of wrinkled black rock that looked as though it had been cut by hand and cemented down in great slabs in this place, with the grooves which the machine – nature in this case – had made in the cutting clearly apparent. Behind me the lines of dry-stone walls, some of the walls as high as six feet, seemed to have been made by nature too. A few times, however, when I went to study them in any detail, I could see that they were pure culture, made with an exquisite sense of order and design, their durability based on a few large stones at regular intervals standing upwards, everything resting subtly on them, all the smaller stones, carefully selected, depending on them.

I found there was a constant need to sit down, and it was easy to find comfortable places in these rocks and observe the simple business of the waves slapping against the rocks further down and sending up spray. There was no need to go on any further. Here was enough. I could lie back on a bed of bare rock with my head resting on my folded-up jacket on a stone for a headrest and notice the yellow lichen on the stones, the wild flowers in the clefts of the rock, the surging of the sea, the smaller island across the sound and the line of horizon. I fell asleep.

The next day was one of those miracle days that you can get in the summer in the west of Ireland. Not a cloud in the sky and the air full of the sweet smell of grass, the stone of the walls making a shadowy chessboard, and the rock in the fields and at the edges of the island seeming darker and more ominous in this brutal sunlight. I did not know what the beach would be like, but knew that you could swim there, so after breakfast I bought some food and took a towel and togs and a book and made for the beach and thought I would stay there for the rest of the day.

It seemed strange to me that such a small island came in so many guises. The houses are built in a long cluster under the shelter and protection of the higher ground in the middle of the island. Nothing is built on the edges of the island. Each stretch I walked had a different configuration of rock, different colours, different height of walls, different sort of lanes between them. I had noticed a beach as I flew over the previous day and knew that it was close to the small airport, but nothing prepared me for this expanse of washed white sand, another world from the black rock of the previous day. What made it look like another planet or, if you had your back to the sea, a stretch of desert was the rise in the middle, like a hump, which gave it an unearthly aura. I found a place to sit among rushes at the back of the beach and I spent the whole day there, reading my book, watching the sea birds, swimming in the ocean a few times, braving the cold waves, and then looking up the few times when a plane flew low in from the mainland and out again. No one else appeared on the beach. It was the sort of day you do not get often in your life.

The actors began to arrive. I noticed them walking from the boat the next morning when I had had my breakfast. Some of them were staying in my lodging house. Soon the weather began to deteriorate and I had to go back for my rainwear and make my way past the church and Dún Chonchúir and the house where Synge had stayed on the island to the spot overlooking the ocean that is called Synge's Chair, which Tim Robinson describes as 'a small structure in which Synge used often to sit, a low, three-quarter-circle wall of massive stones on the brink of the highest cliff of Inis Meáin, still called Cathaoir Synge, "Synge's Chair". It is obviously ancient but its original purpose is not clear, though probably it was some sort of look-out post.'

Soon the road gave way to a path which was made of tarmacadam and seemed newly made. The mist was coming heavy now; there was only greyness ahead. Synge wrote about these great shifts in weather: 'the continual passing in this island between the misery of last night and the splendour of today seems to create an affinity between the moods of these people and the moods of varying rapture and dismay that are frequent in artists and in certain forms of alienation.' I had instead to deal with the splendour of yesterday, not a cloud nor a whisper of wind even when night had fallen, and then with this lapse into mist and wind and rain. I made my way back to the public house where I spent a few hours before going home to read.

That night the mist held up but the rain kept off and many of the islanders made their way to the parish hall to see Synge's two short plays *In the Shadow of the Glen* and *Riders to the Sea*. What is so strange about the second of these plays is how much is left out; there is only talk of the danger, the weather and drowned. What

Tim Robinson noticed adds a starkness to the drama – all points of the compass bring doom in their wake: the body washed up in the north, the great roaring in the west, the wind rising from the south.

There was silence in the hall when Marie Mullen appeared on the stage, a grace in her slow movements, her face expressionless. Her son's body had been washed up in the north and now her other son was going out to be drowned. She needed to move between a pure realism in her tone and someone enacting a ritual, she had to allow her lines to include both the rhythms of ordinary speech and the sounds of a howl of despair. None of us could take our eyes off her as she moved towards her final speeches intoning the names of the drowned and how the news had come to her each time. There was a great humility and a resignation in her tone as well as a depth of grandeur. I know these lines off by heart. I had come to the island to hear them said. But there were a few moments in that small hall among the islanders when I would have wished for anything to happen but the last son Bartley to be drowned, when I was caught up in the immediacy of the drama, hoping that what was ready to unfold, in all its inevitable tragedy, would not happen, could somehow be prevented. And then she spoke the lines. She told us what she saw and the short masterpiece, which had taken root in Synge's imagination not far from here a hundred years before, came to its conclusion: 'Michael has a clean burial in the far north, by the grace of the Almighty God. Bartley will have a fine coffin out of the white boards, and a deep grave surely. What more can we want than that? No man at all can be living for ever, and we must be satisfied.'

The following year I came back to the island. It was July and the arctic terns governed the white beach like sentinels, swooping low and angrily over anyone who walked there, anyone who might pose a threat to their eggs which were laid in the sand. Once more the weather changed drastically, from the first afternoon when planes could not fly to the days afterwards, which were soft and warm. I walked to the places I had been before, watching the sea and the rock and the astonishing range of wildflowers in the fields and in the clefts between the rocks. Some of the old paths between the dry-stone walls were magnificent. I was using the detailed map which Tim Robinson had made of the island, where each path is marked and many are named and all the monuments and houses are included, with more than sixty names in Irish for parts of the coast of the island.

Soon, I put the map away and followed my nose again, finding paths and places to sit and lie, moving as close to the edge as I thought safe. In my meanderings, I never found Synge's Chair. I came close to it on two sides and thought maybe it was merely a few stones you could rest against, but nothing that was easy to identify. On one of the evenings I mentioned this to my hosts, who must have realized from what I said that I had missed, through laziness and lack of knowledge and following the wrong paths, a crucial dramatic stretch of the coast of Inis Meáin. They were too polite, however, to tell me. Instead, the woman of the house, Áine de Blacam, who is from the island, said she would take me on a walk the next day. She loved walking the island, she said, but I knew she was busy, and I was grateful for her time.

We set out to walk over the hill of the island, past Dún Chonchúir, to the west side, which had a view of some of the cliffs of Árainn, the largest island. It had been raining earlier, but the day had cleared, although the sky was dark and grey. The path between small fields was easy. I could not understand why I had not found it before. The coast, as we moved along bare rock, was much more dramatic here, the sea more fierce. This was not a place you could easily fall asleep. We watched the waves coming from far out, looking for a high one, which would cut under the rock and emerge in a vast spray from one of the blow holes in the rock. It was easy to imagine how vulnerable a currach, made just of tarred canvas stretched over a framework of laths and timbers, would be against the merciless weight of this sea and the sheer height of the rocks. We stood back and watched as waves smashed against the cliff and then poured under with enormous rage to spurt up through the holes in the rock.

What we came to next frightened me and amazed me. Huge rocks, weighing many tons, lay scattered on the bare rock. I realized that they had been hurled over the cliff by the power of the waves in a number of fierce winter storms. They had been broken from the cliff by the sea, held in the ocean's fretful arms for a time, washed of some of their colour and then let sink. The rocks were kept in waiting on the ocean's bed. It is hard to imagine what it must have been like on those nights, or days that must have seemed like nights, when the tide was full and the storm coming from the Atlantic was beyond belief and there was no protection at all. A time when the sea could do anything, including shift a huge piece of rock from the deep and lift it, deposit it powerfully, wilfully in one swoop on the edge of the cliff like something falling from the sky.

It was a warning to the world in case any of us would ever come to underestimate the sea's great force, its implacable and cruel ownership of the world. The sea made clear to us that day that it had merely lent us the cliff for a time to walk on and observe. It would come back, as each wave, low now on this summer afternoon, would return, to threaten and to warn.

And just beyond this then was the chair the great writer had used to observe the sea birds and the sea. He had brought his notebook here and his well-stocked mind. It was much higher than a chair, more like a roofless observation post in dry stone. After the sheer flamboyance of what we had witnessed, this was a gentle place, easy to sit in, a place to sleep in on a summer's day. Despite the turbulence all around, it had remained in place. We stood in its shelter and looked out at the waves. Soon we would walk back along the paths to the middle of the island where the houses were.

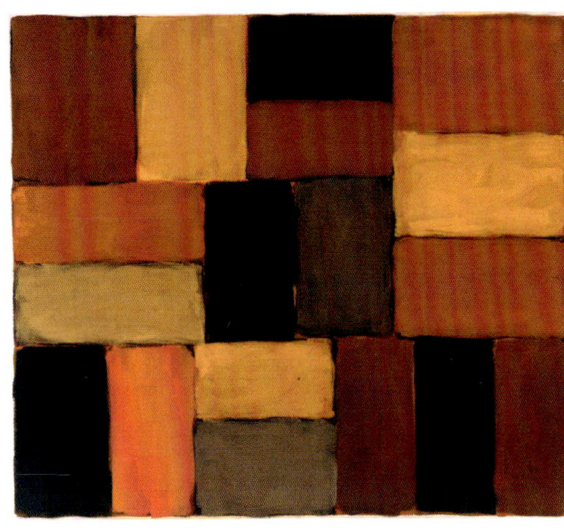

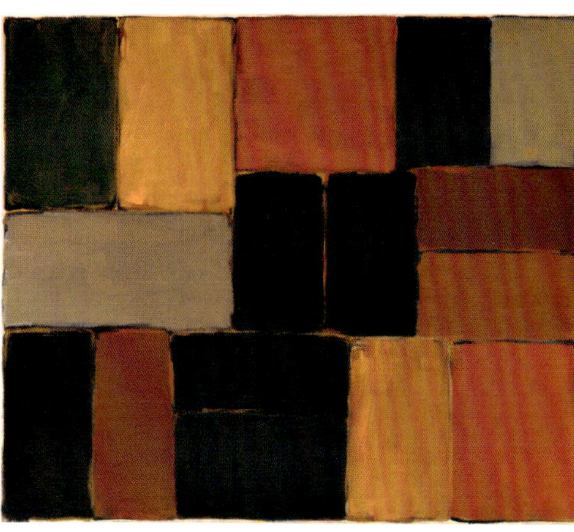

Inis Meáin

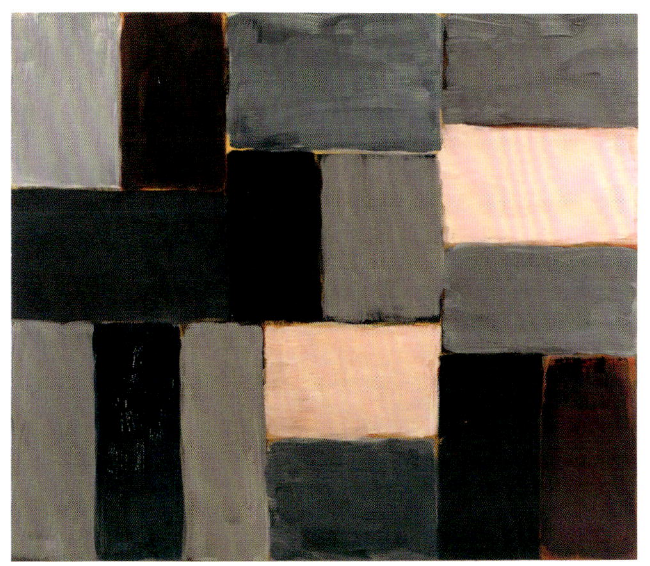

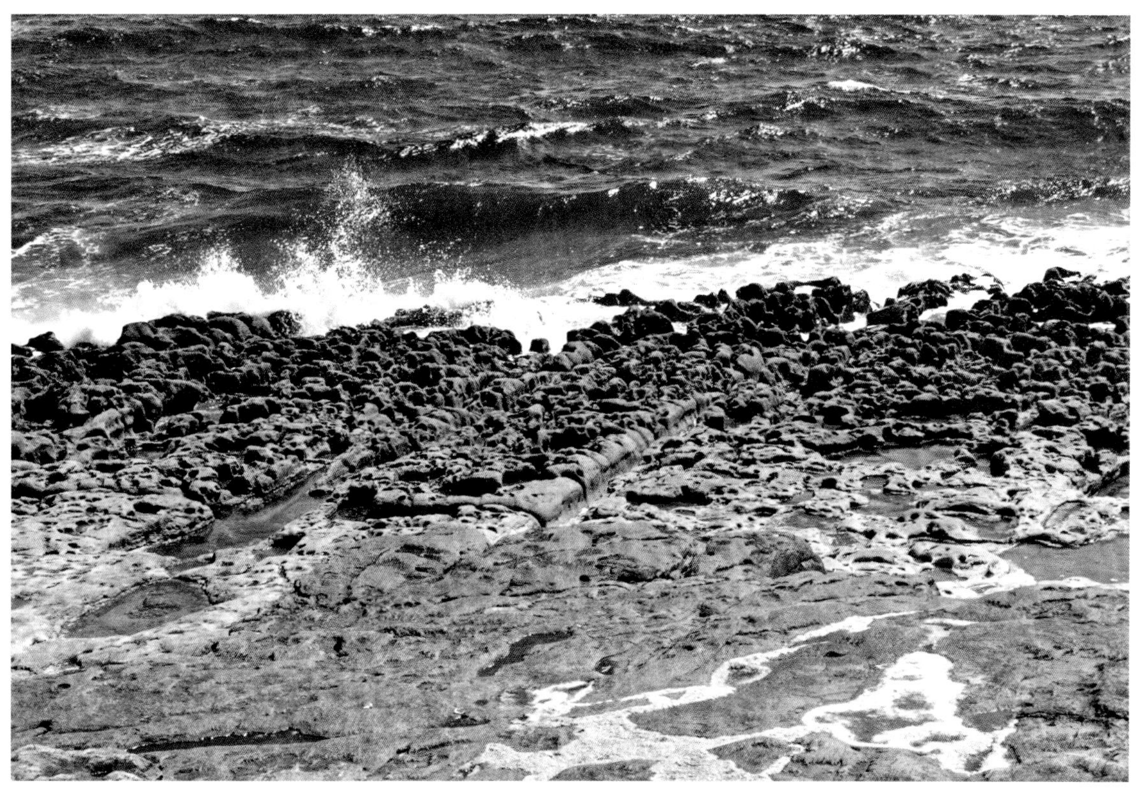

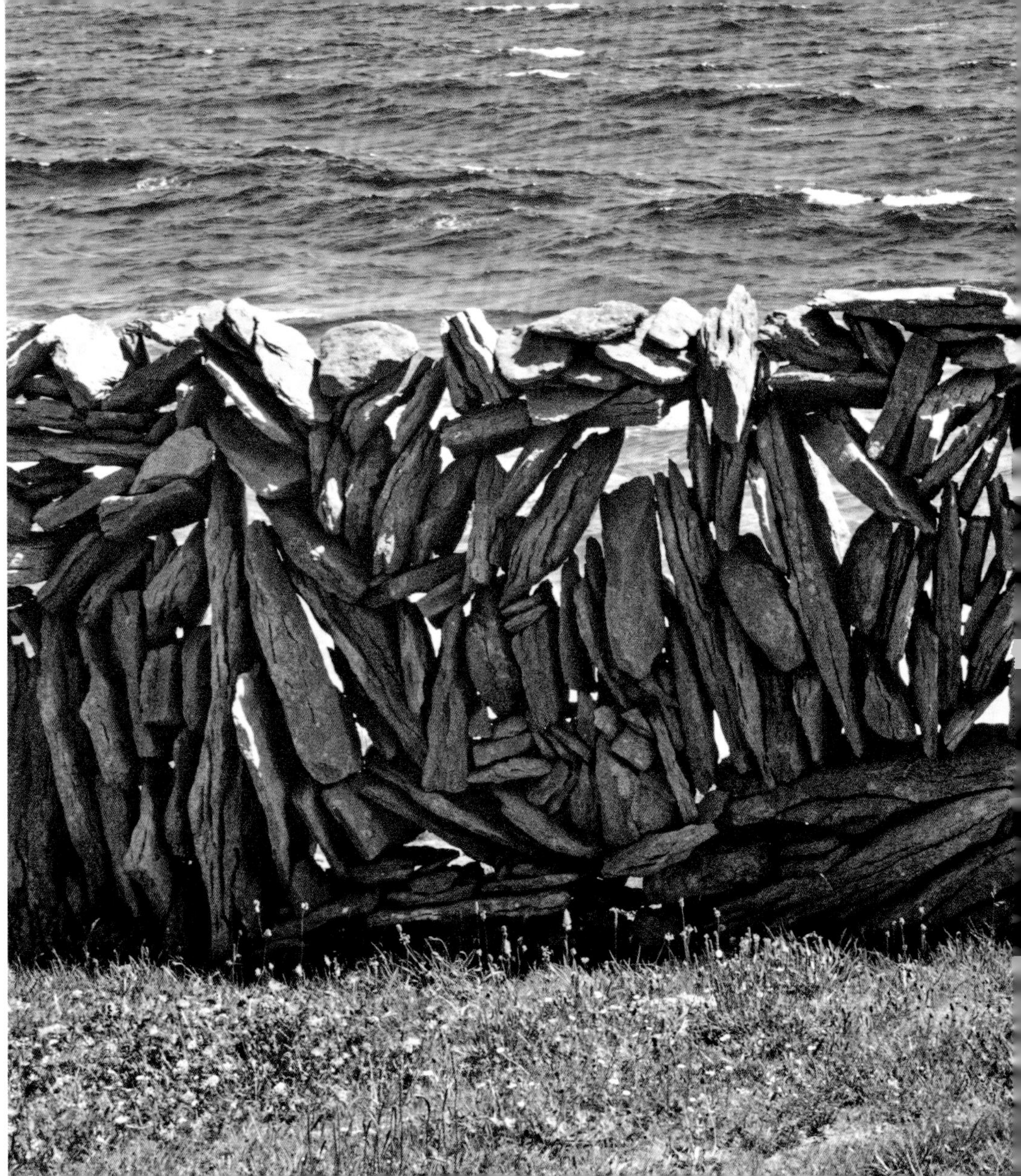

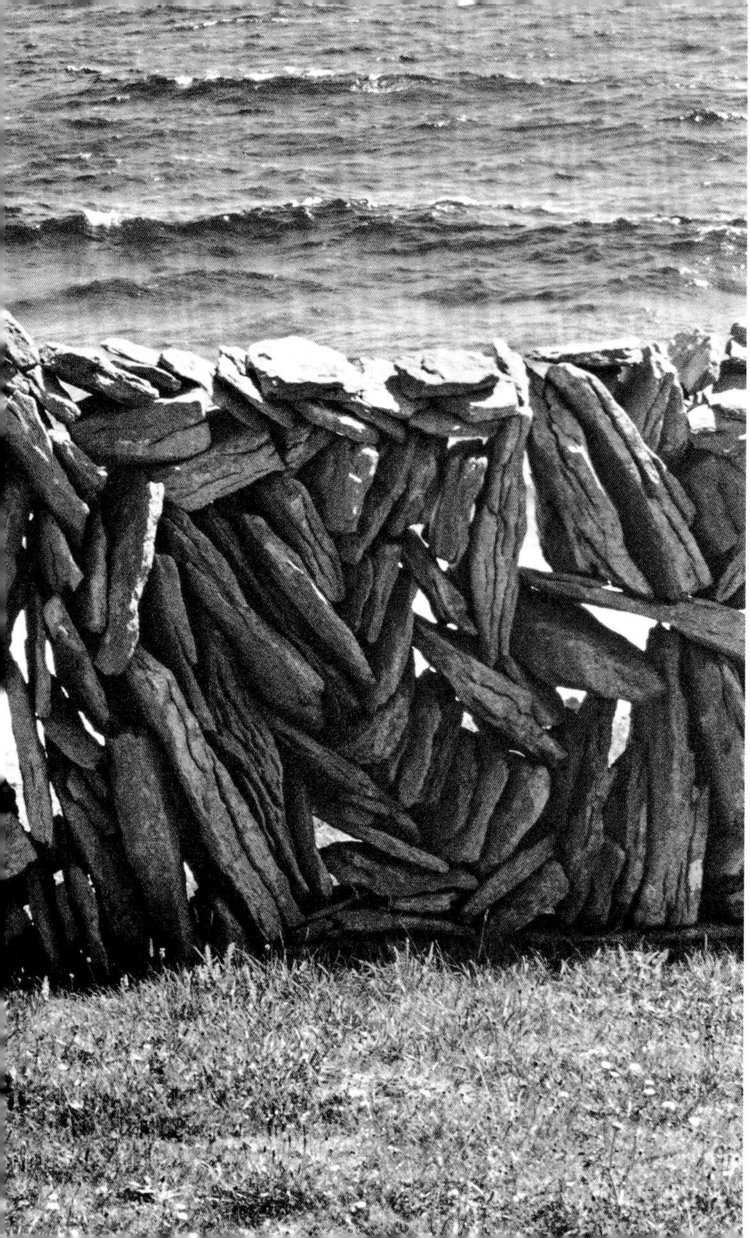

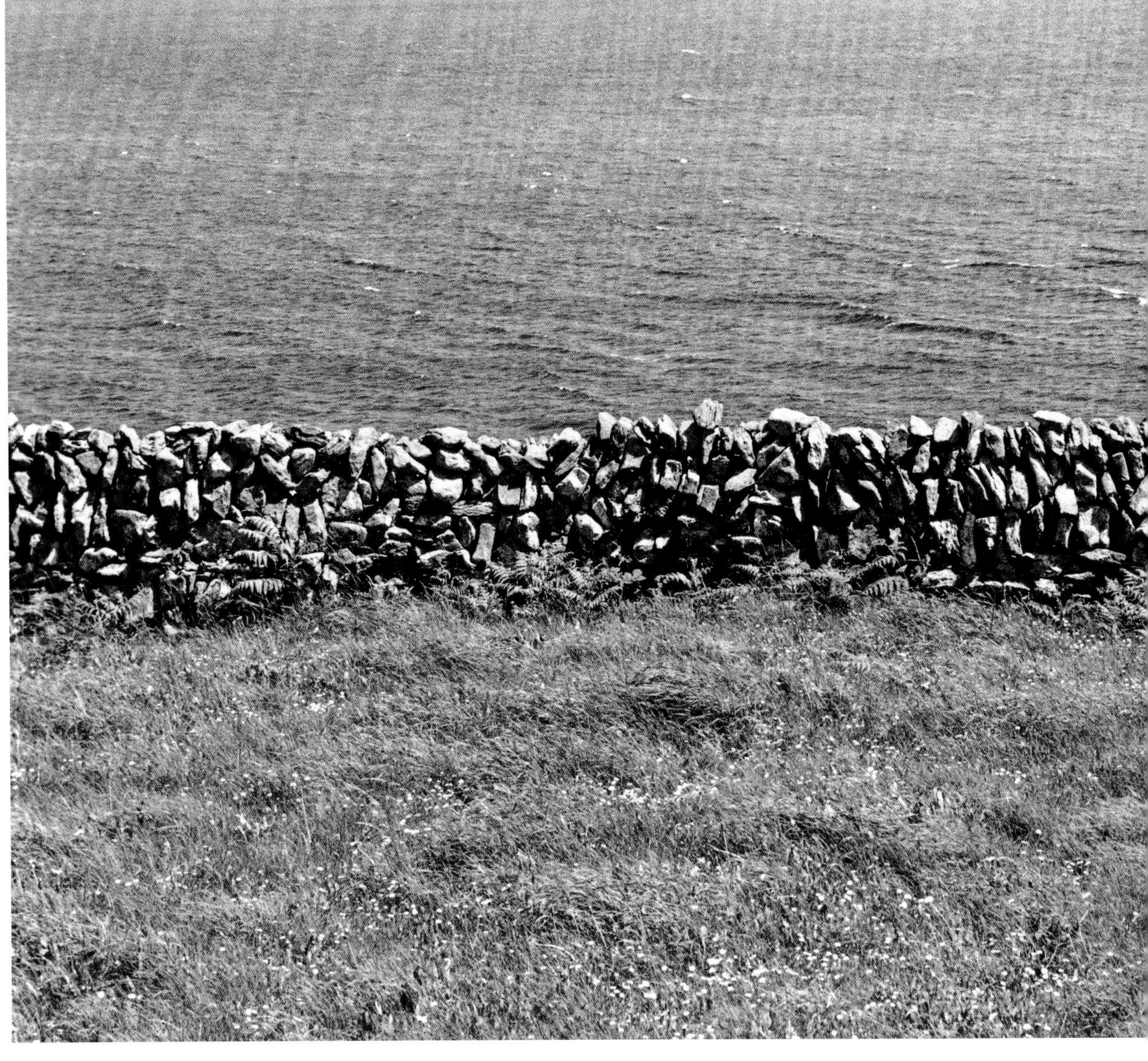

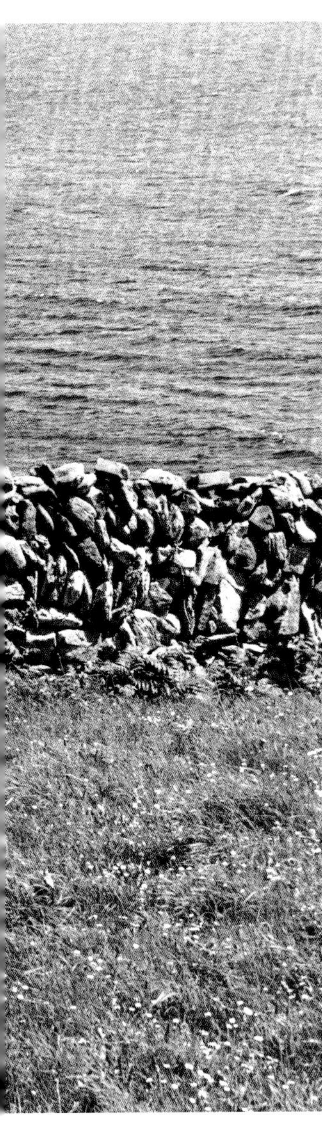

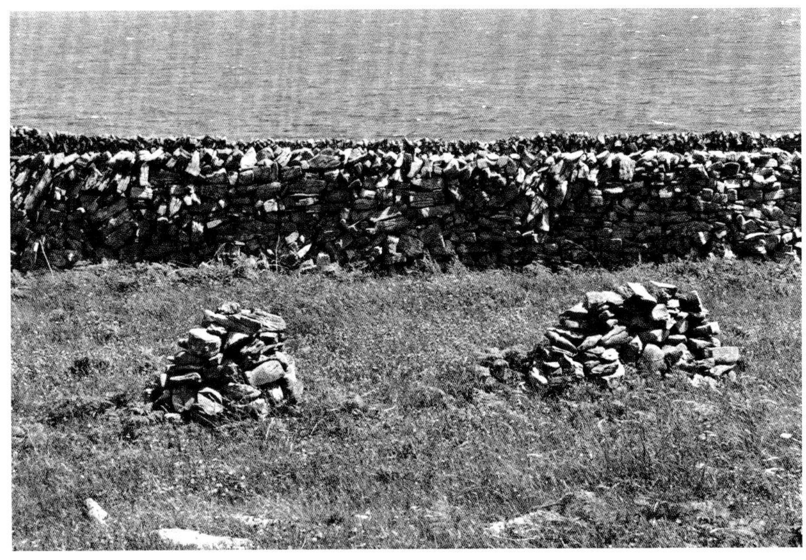

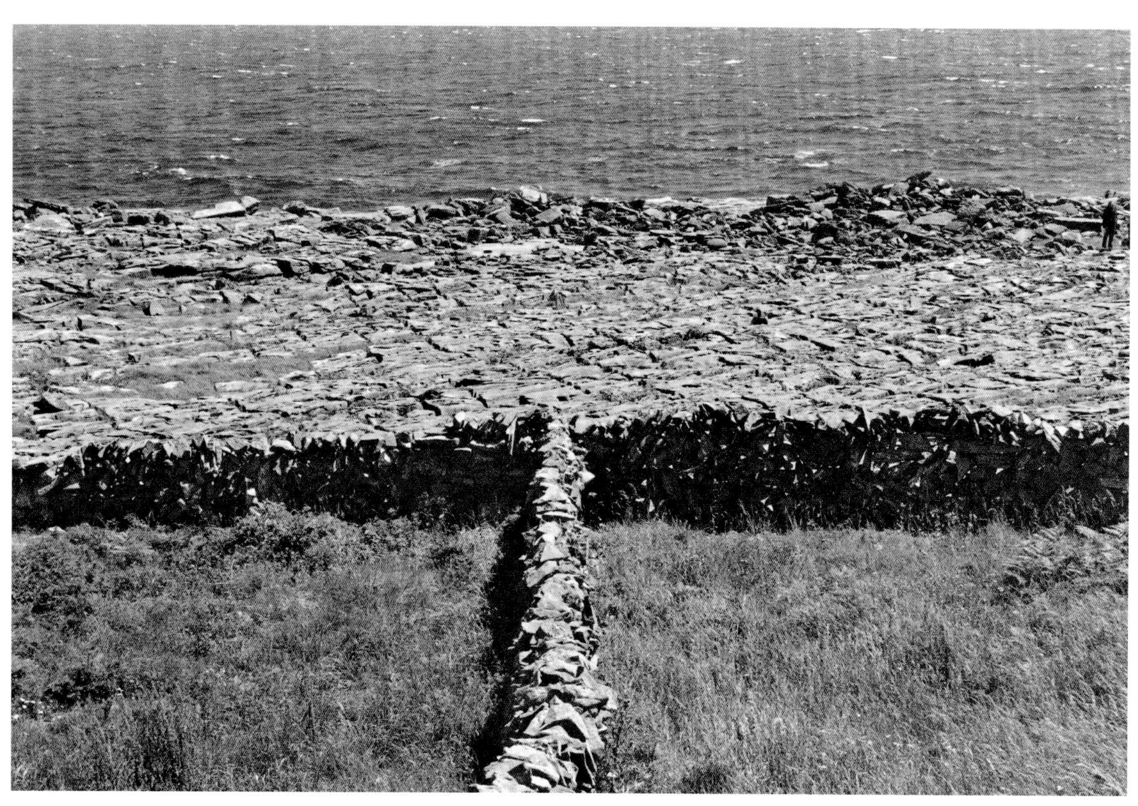

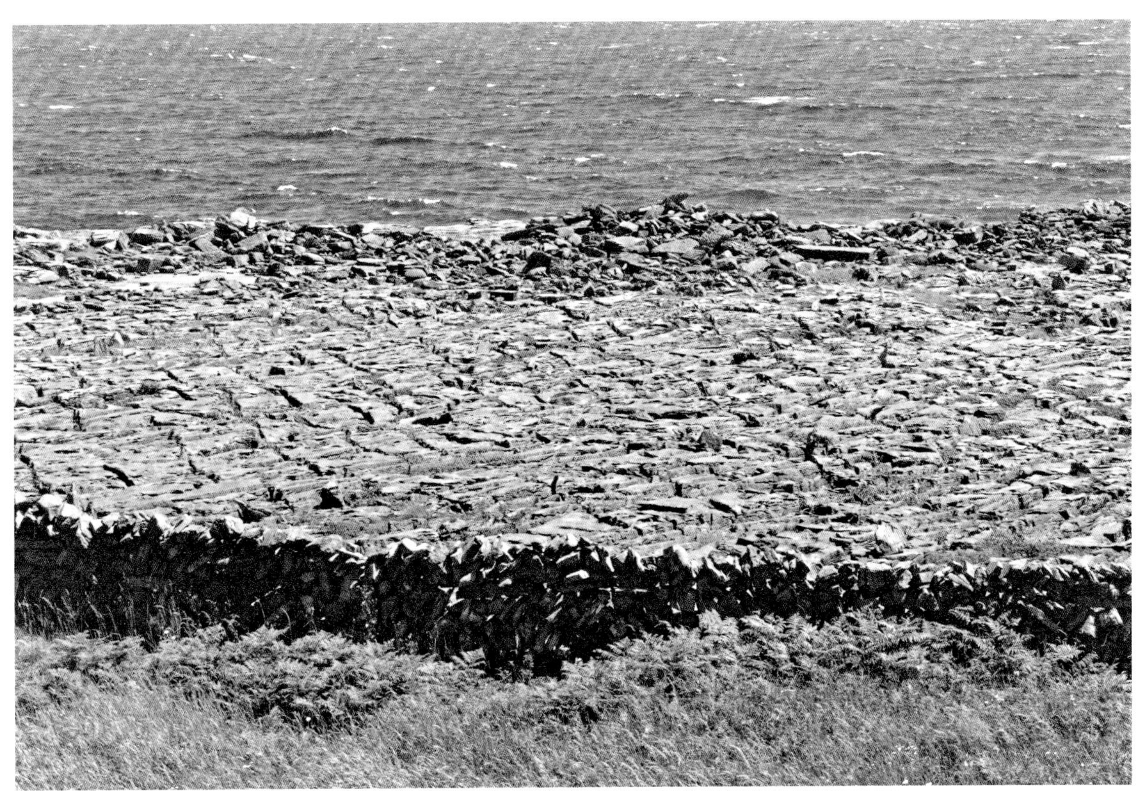

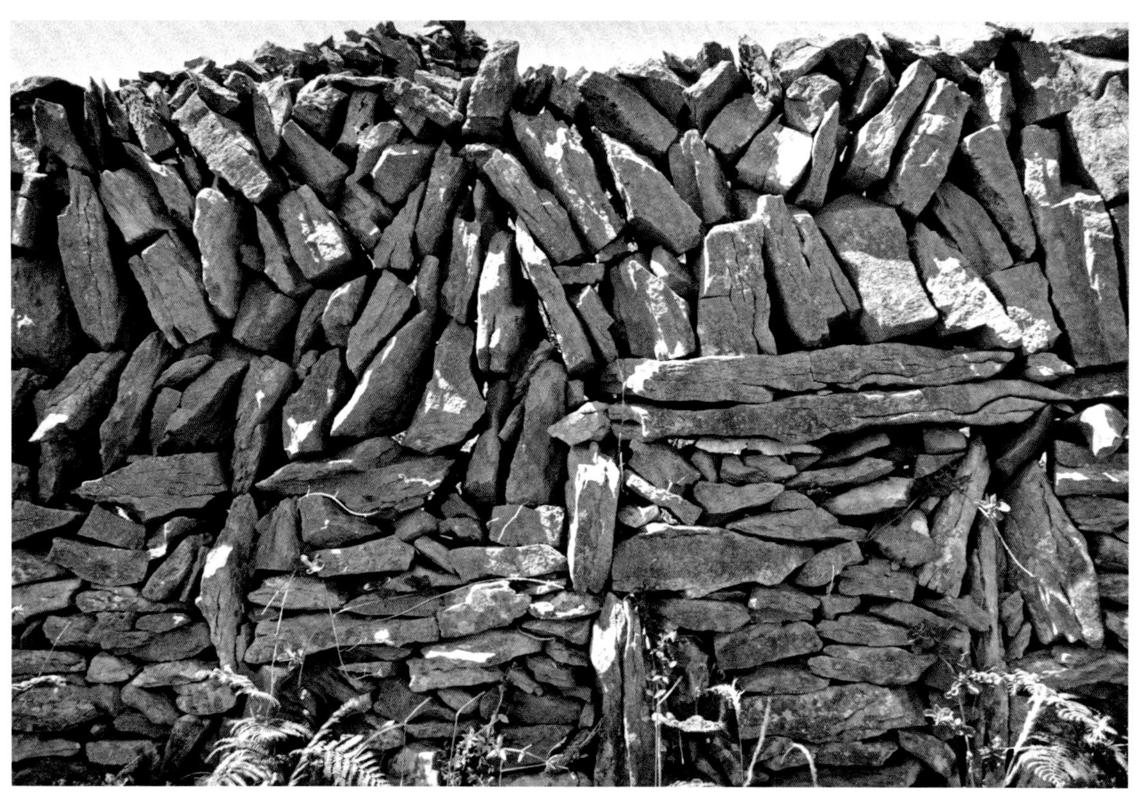

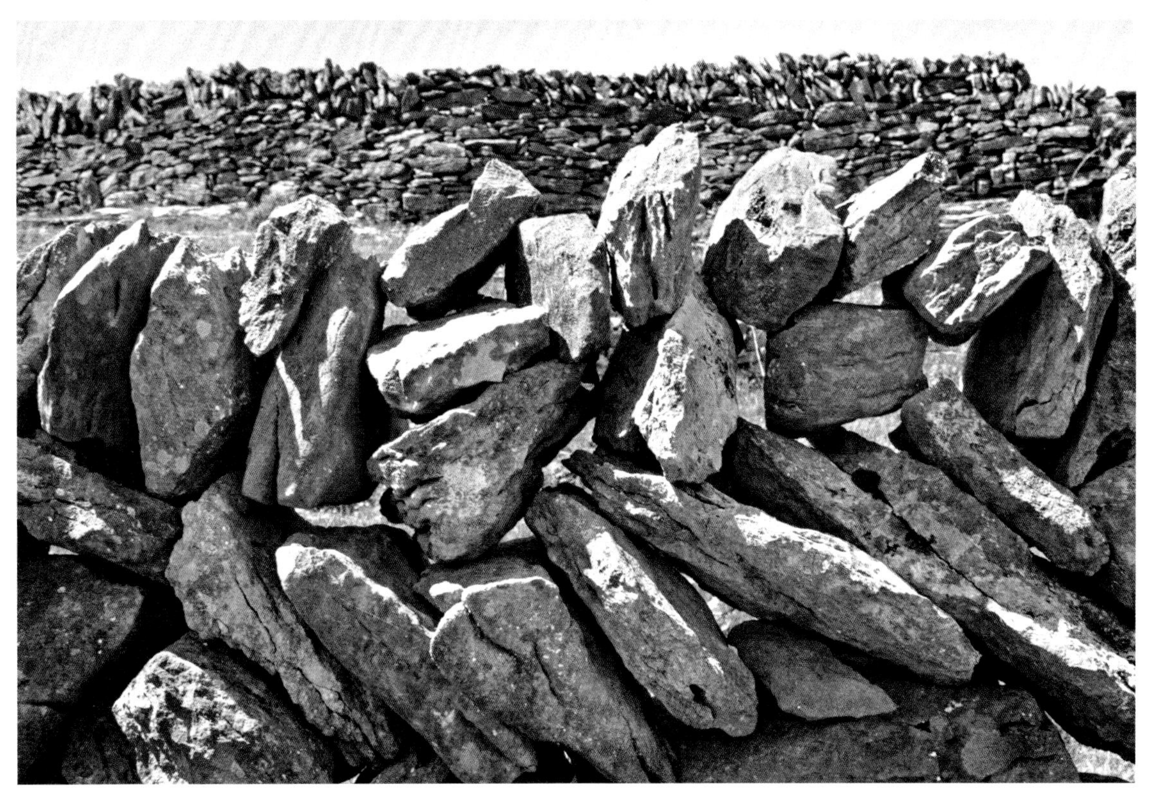

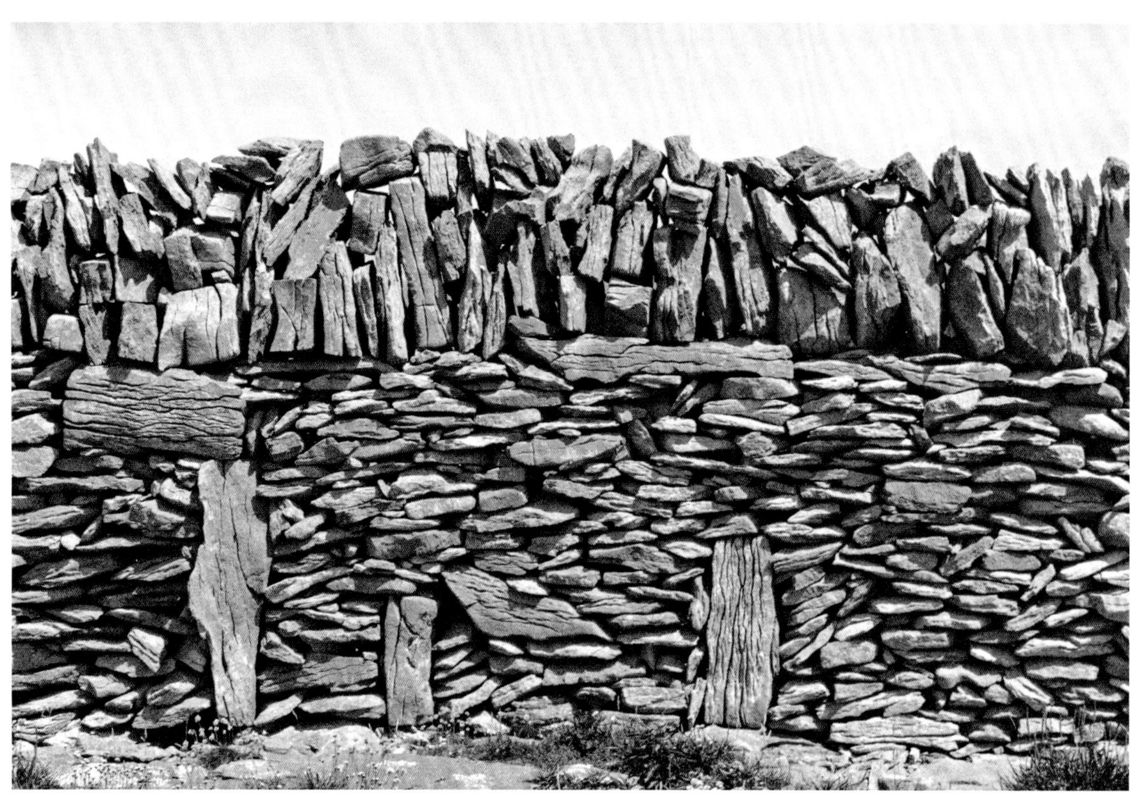

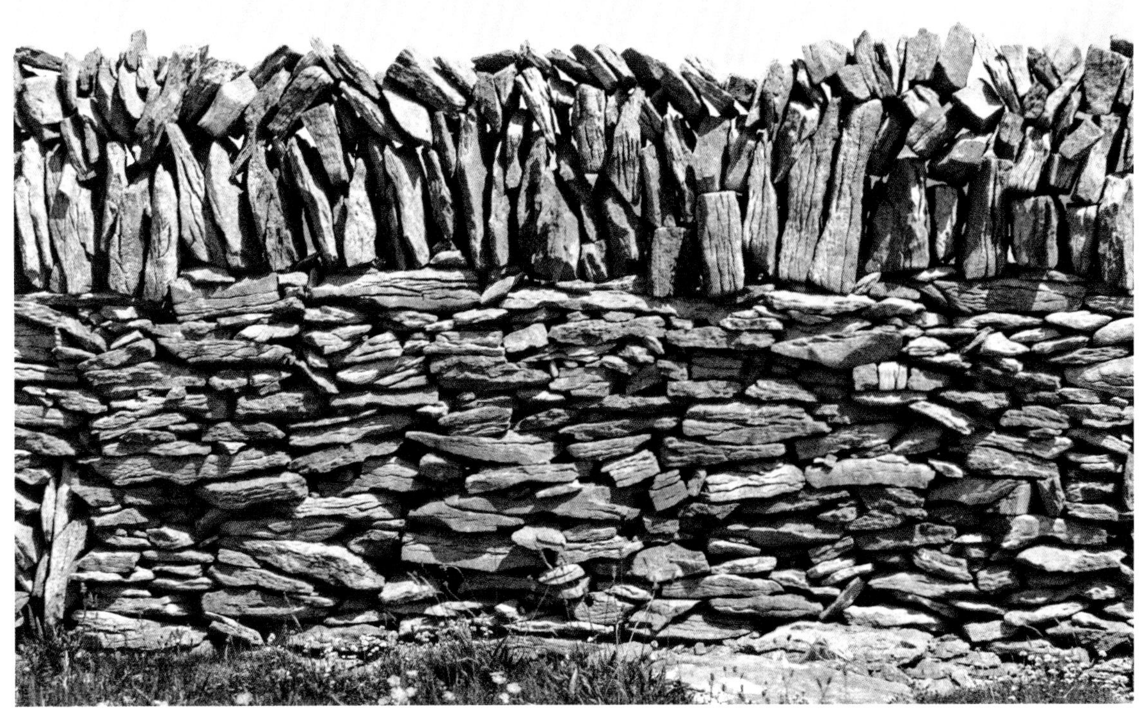

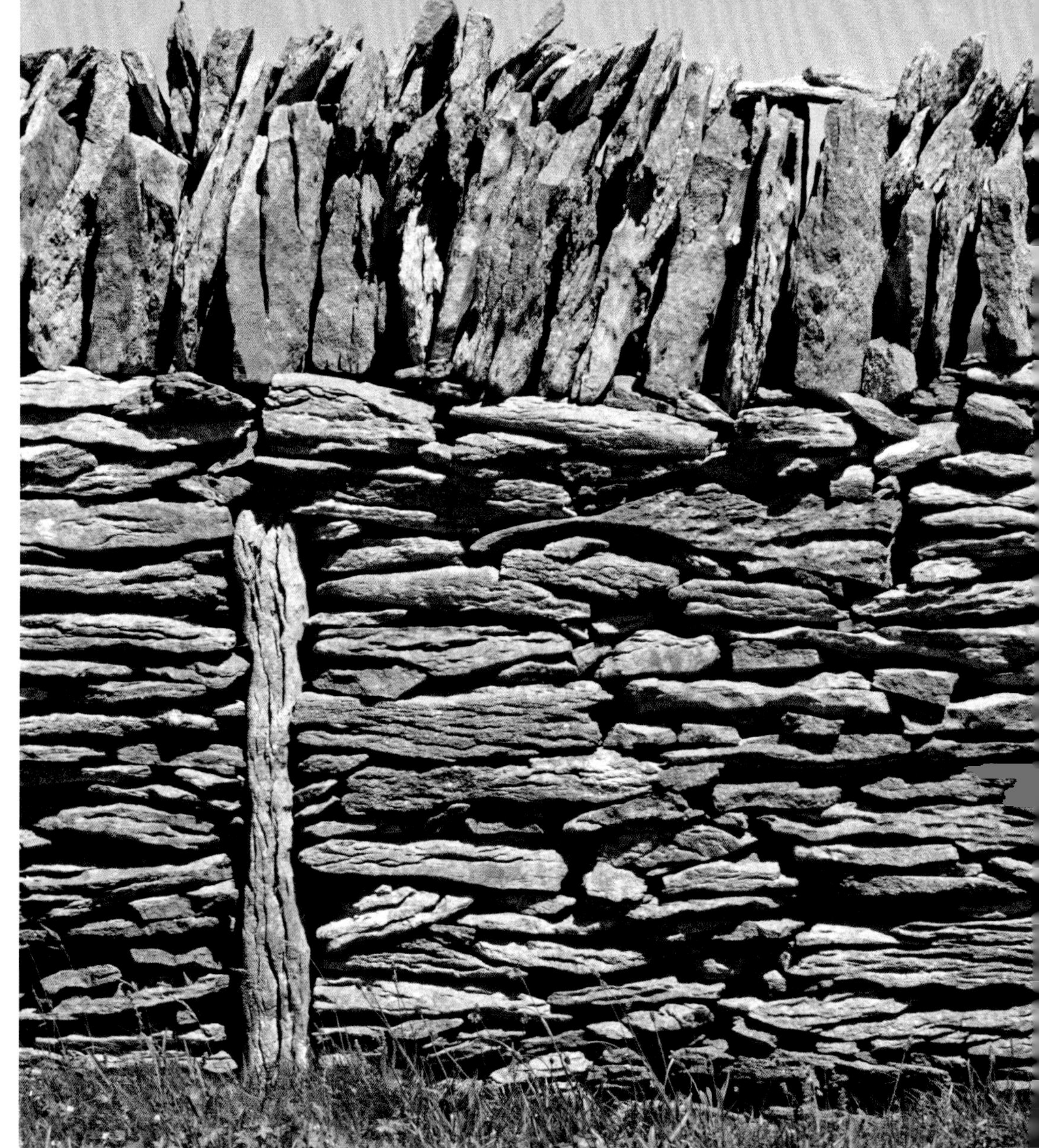

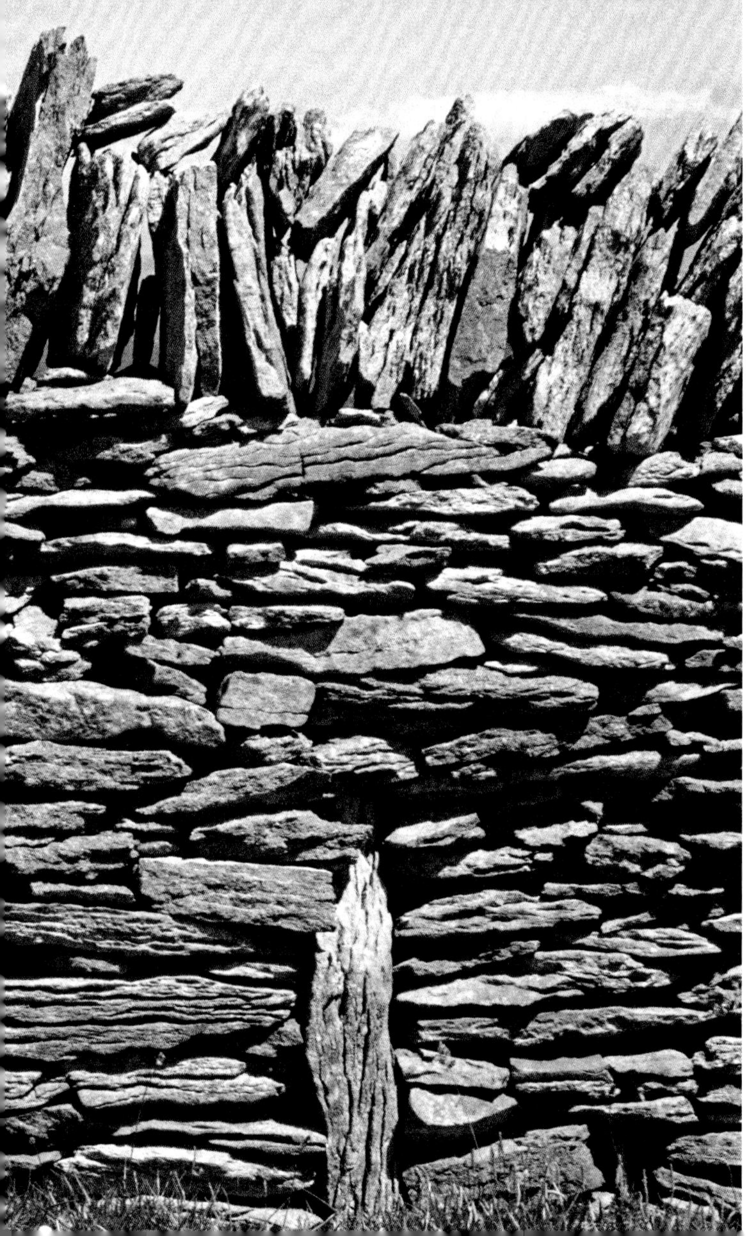

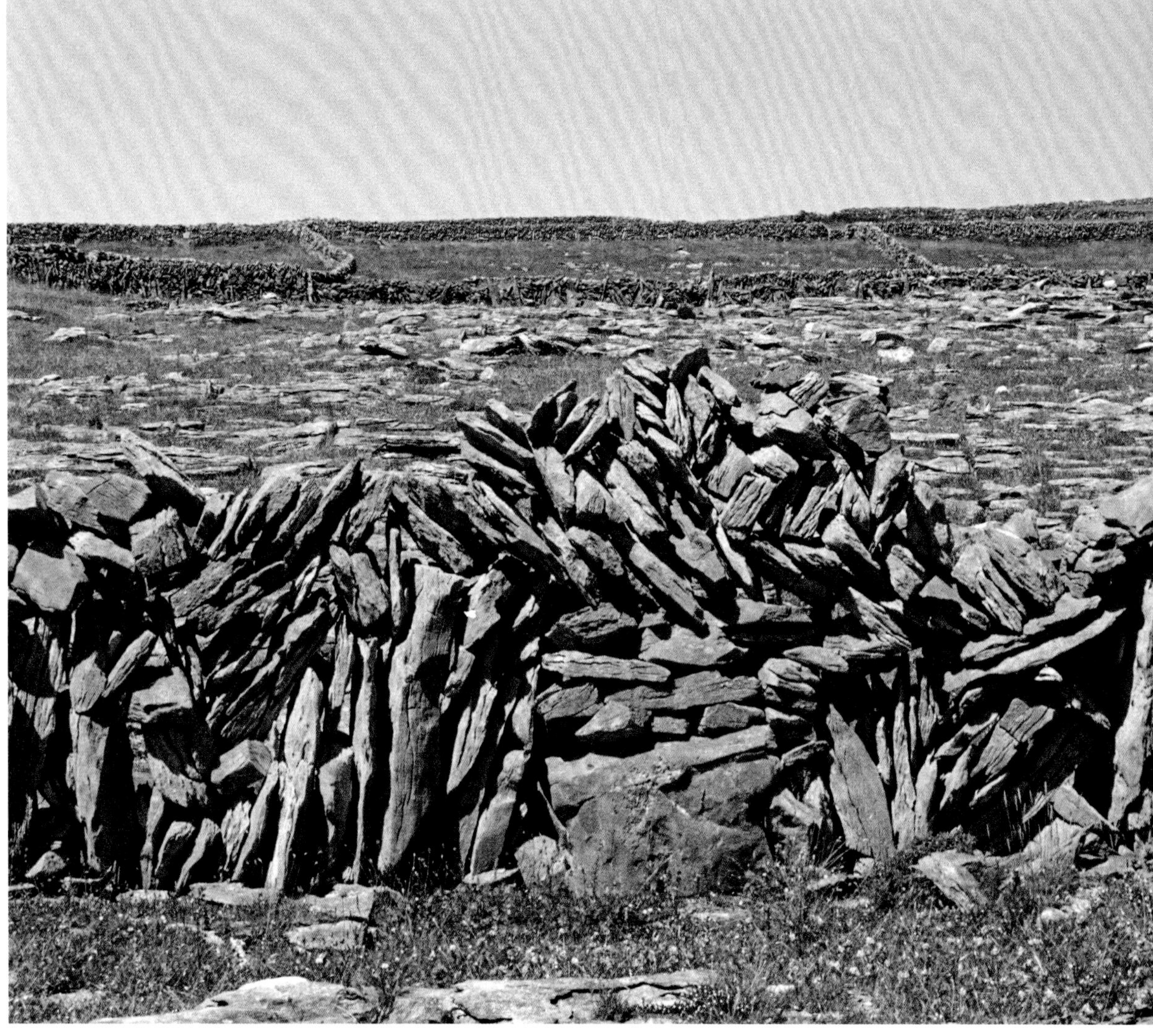

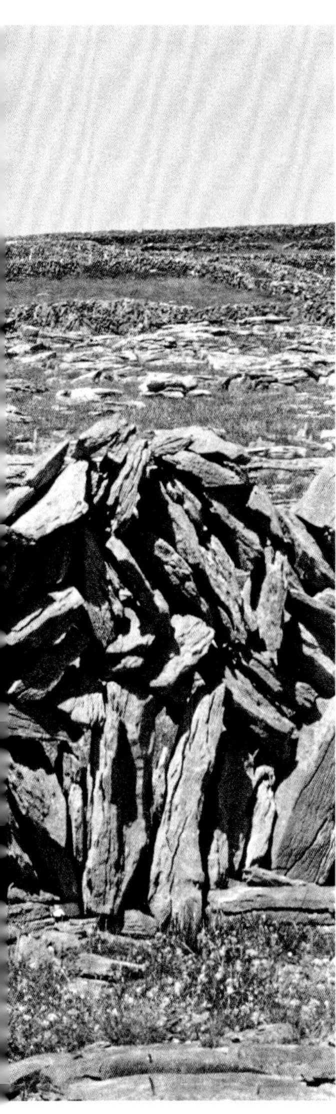

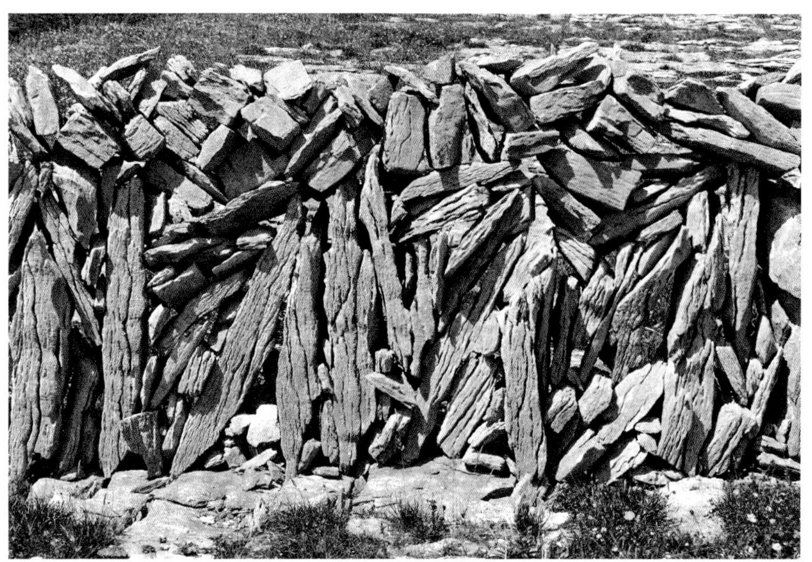

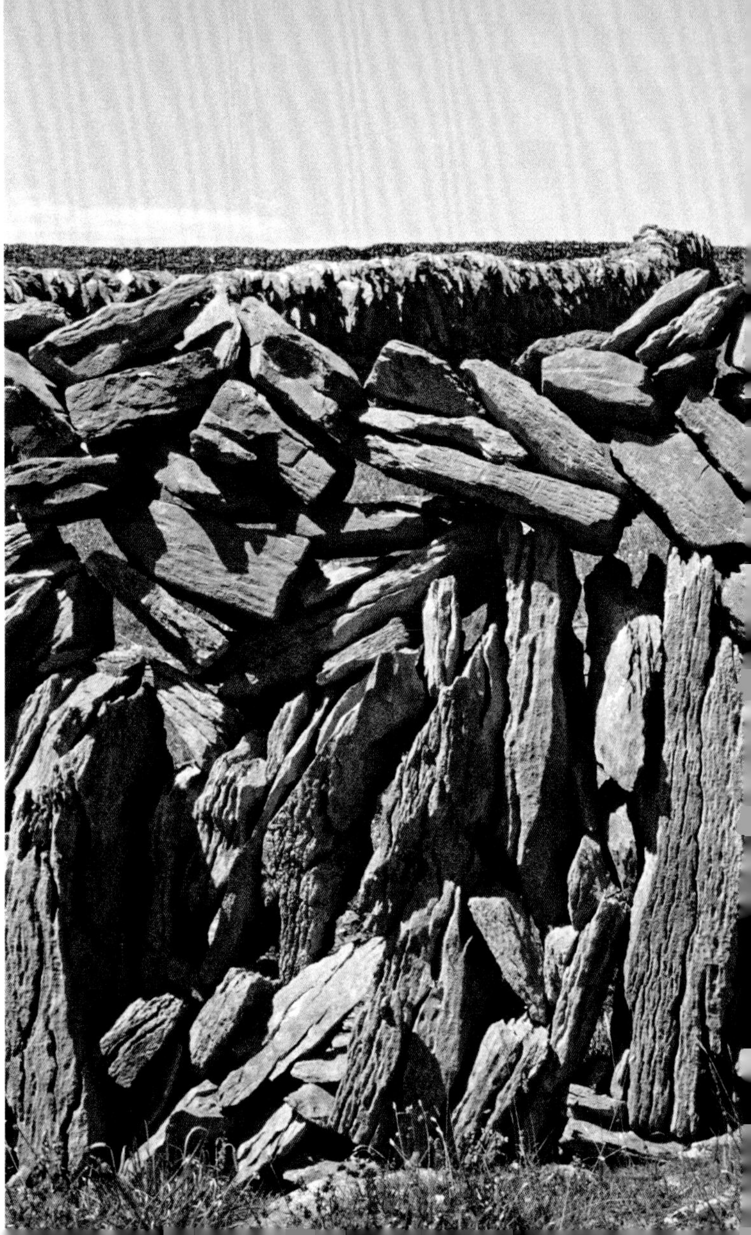

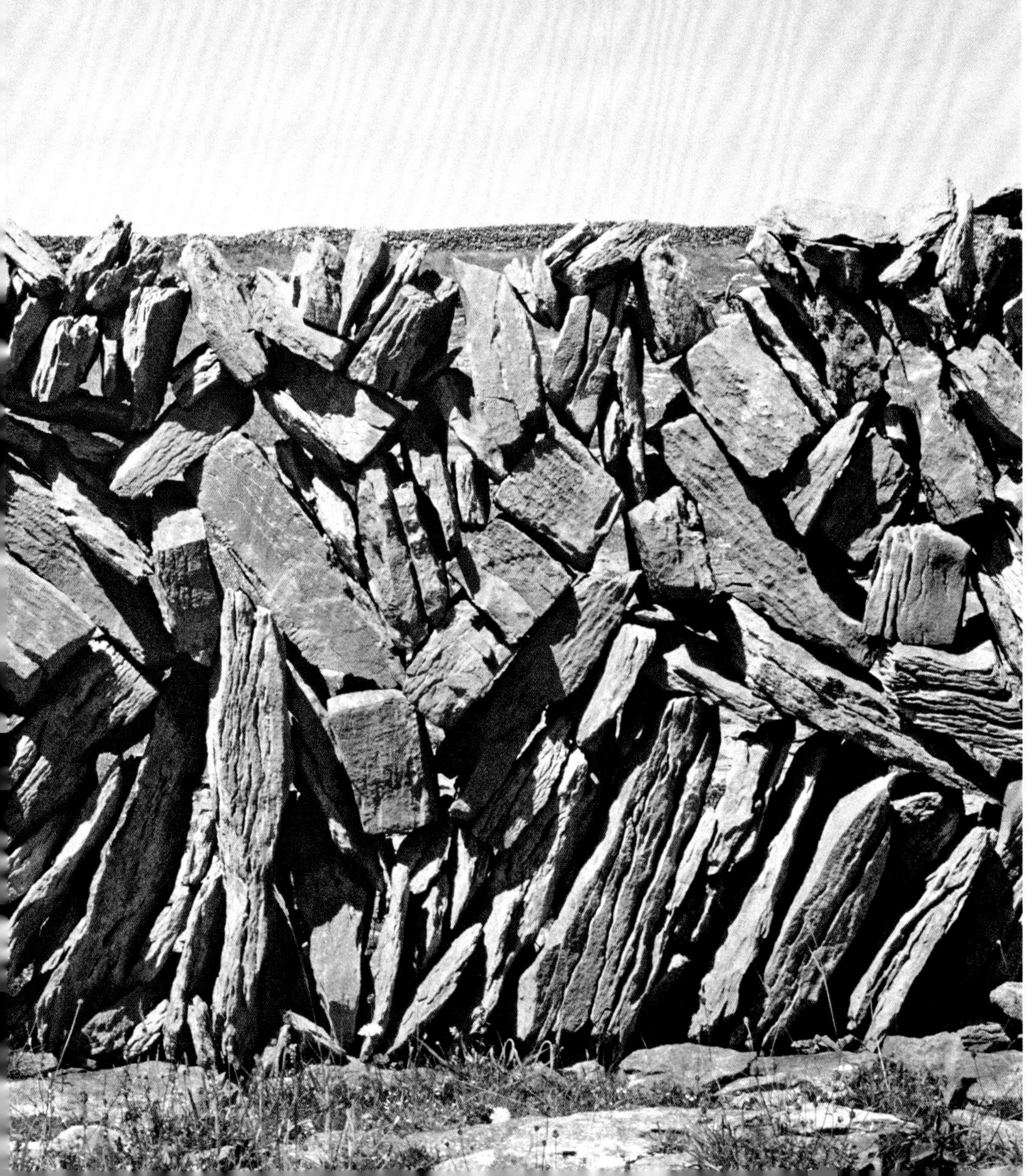

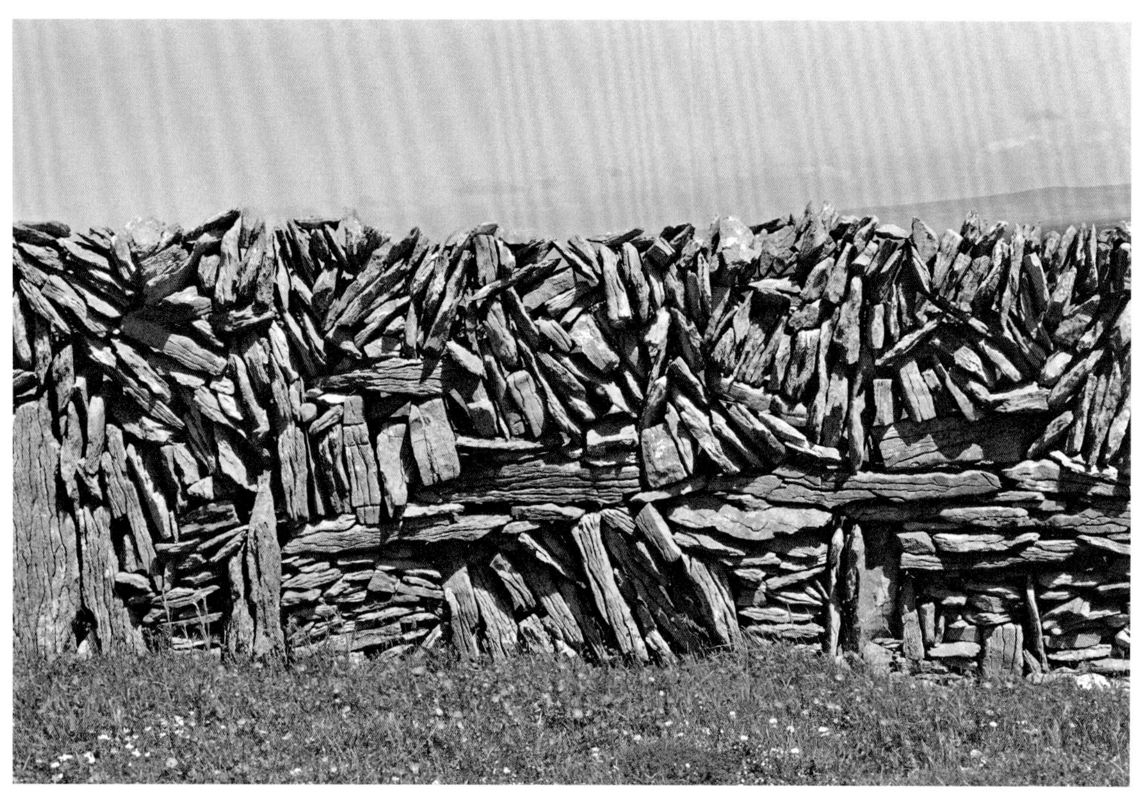

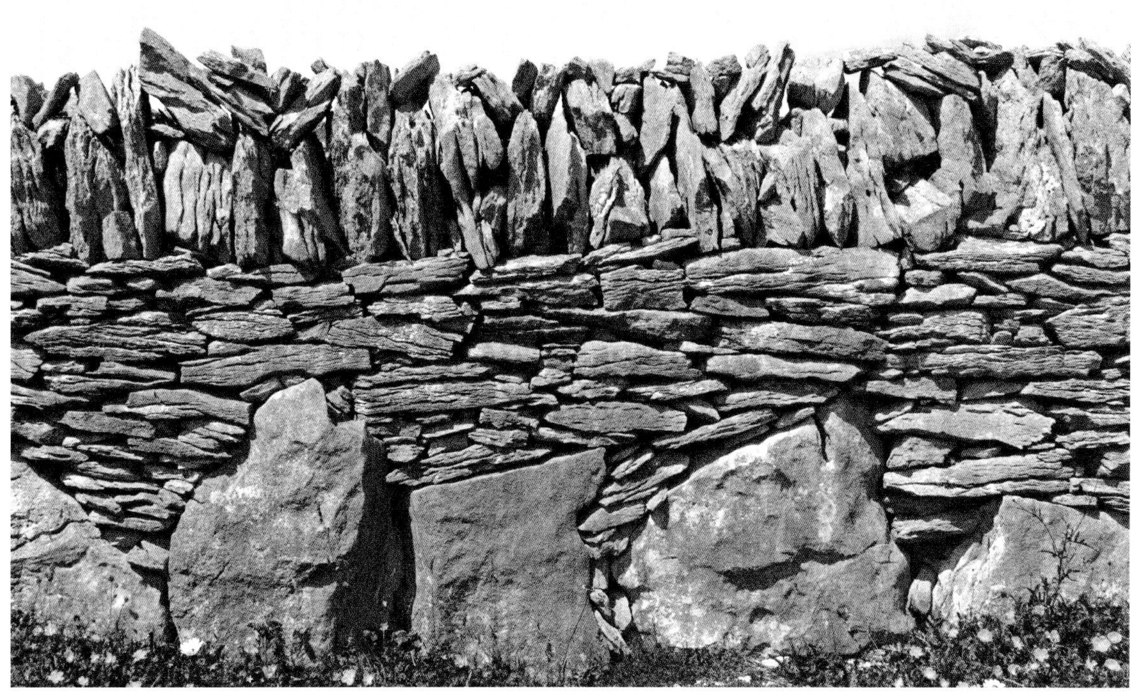

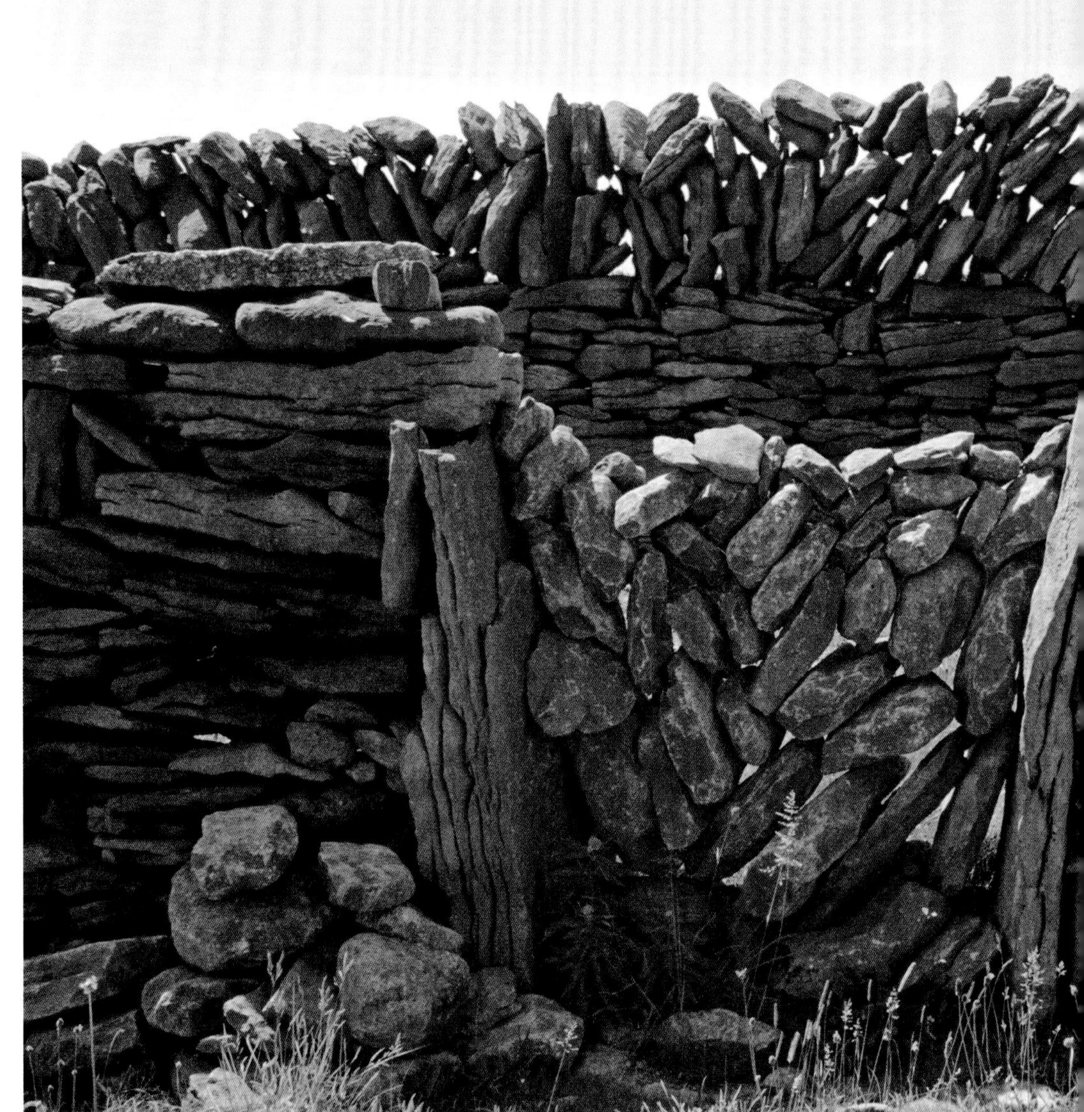

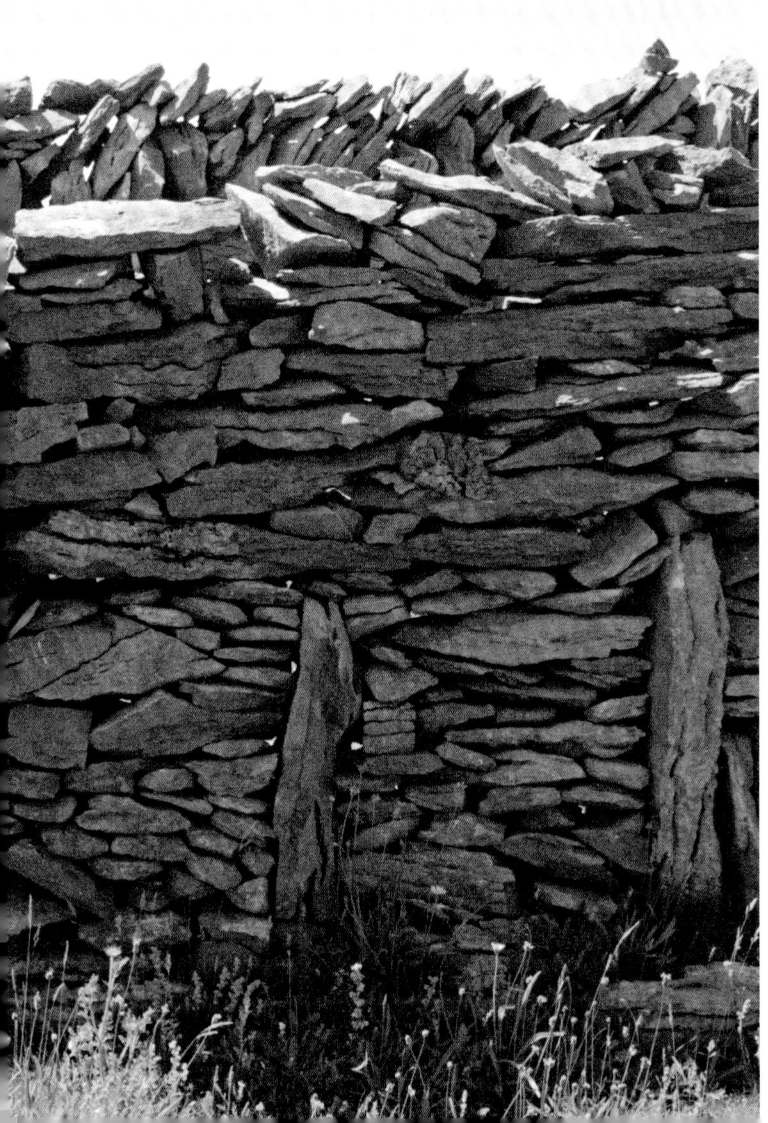

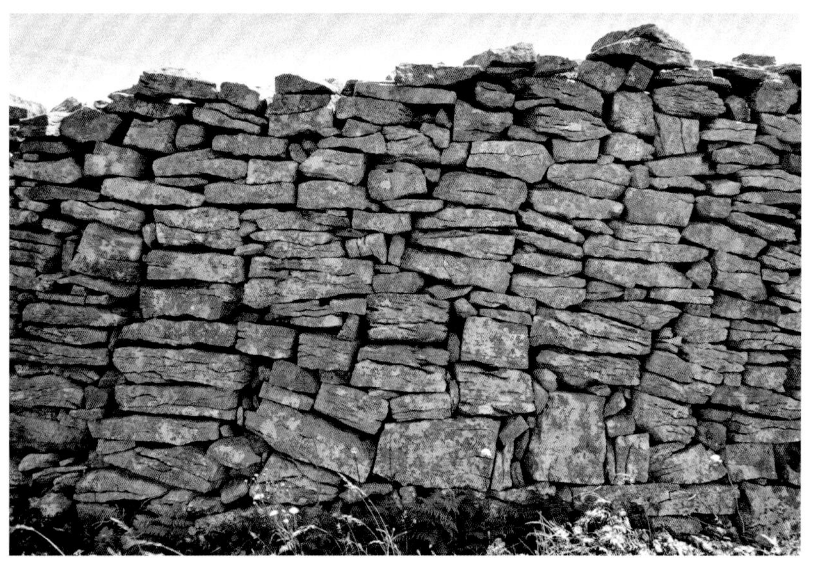

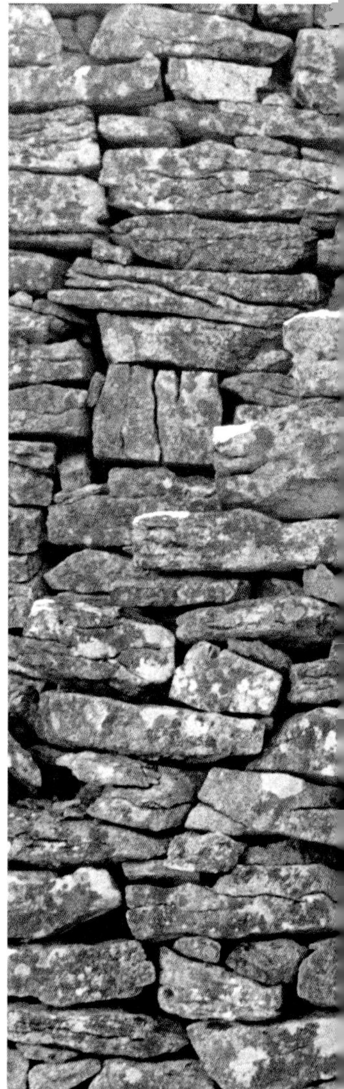

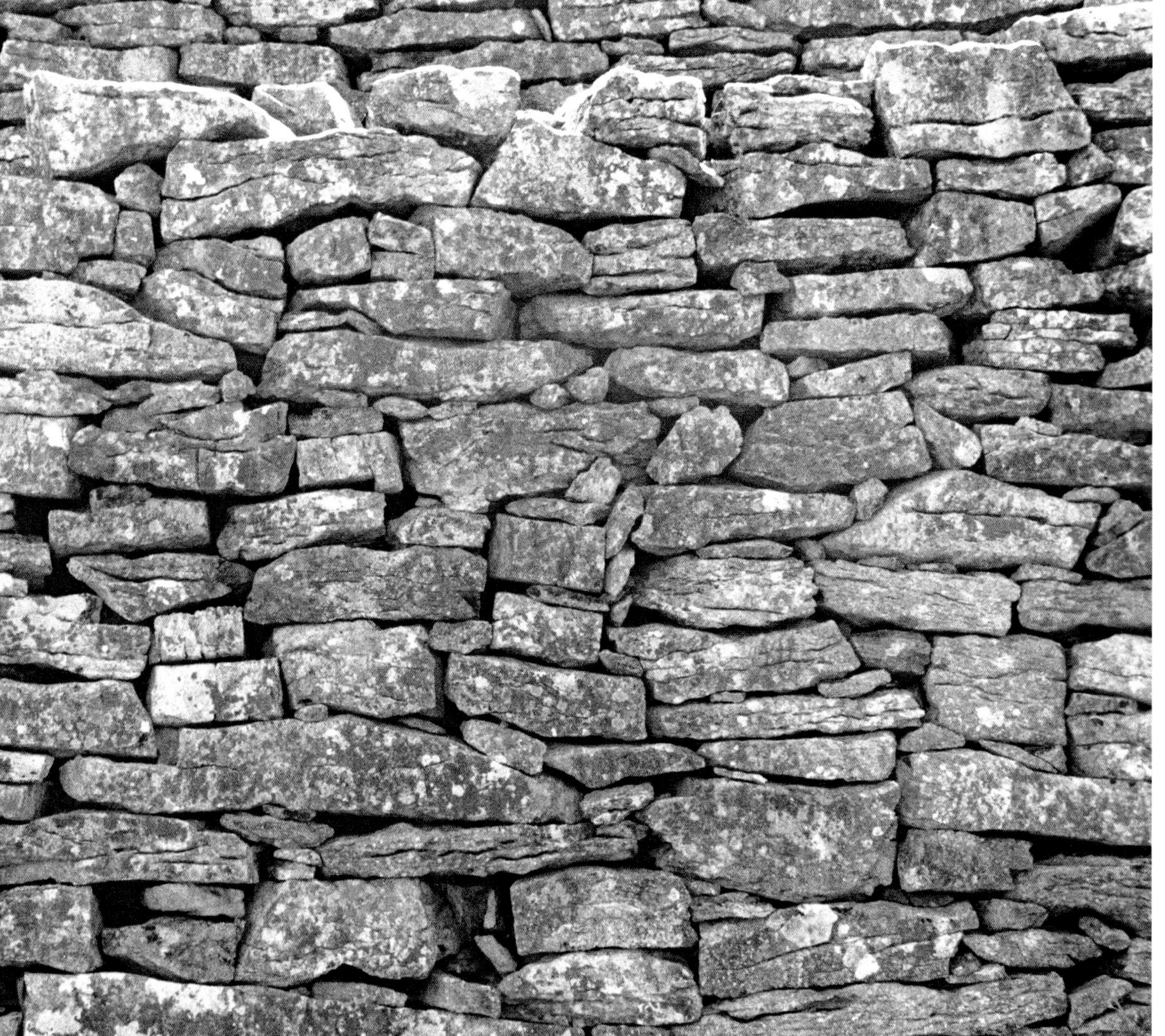

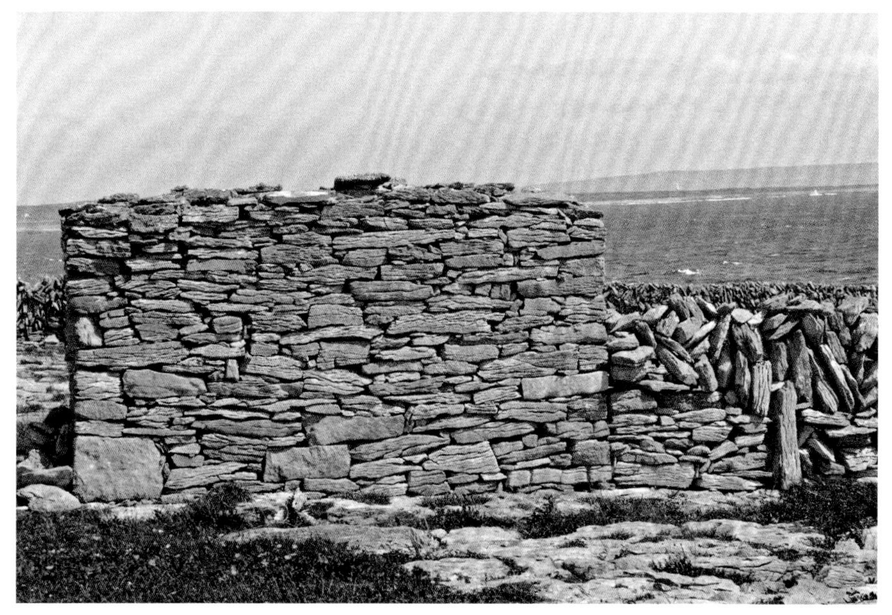

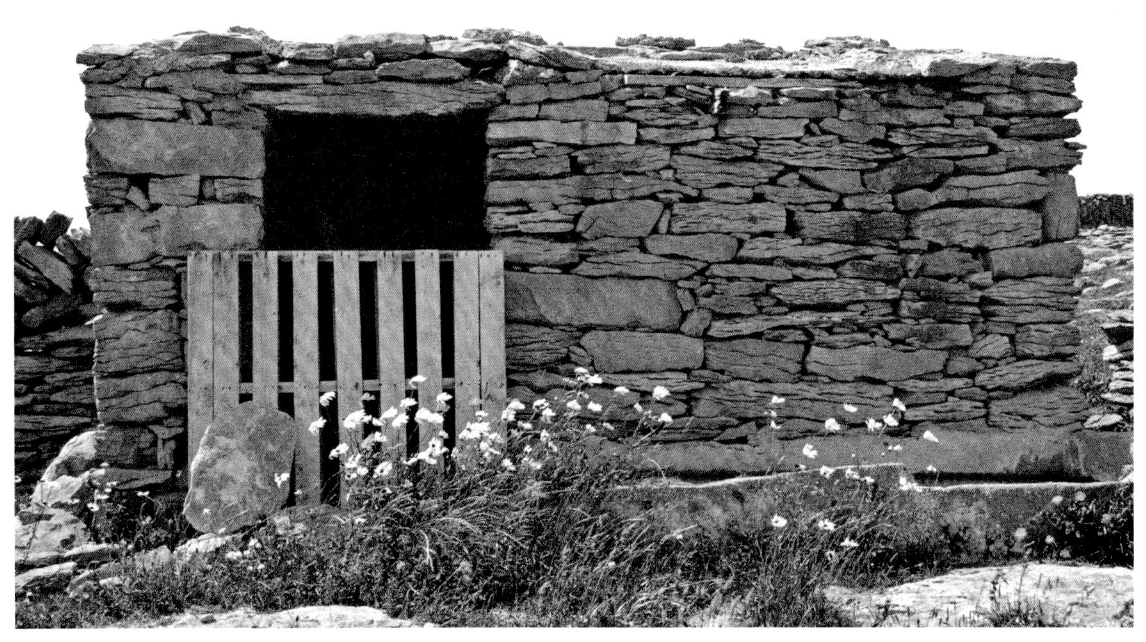

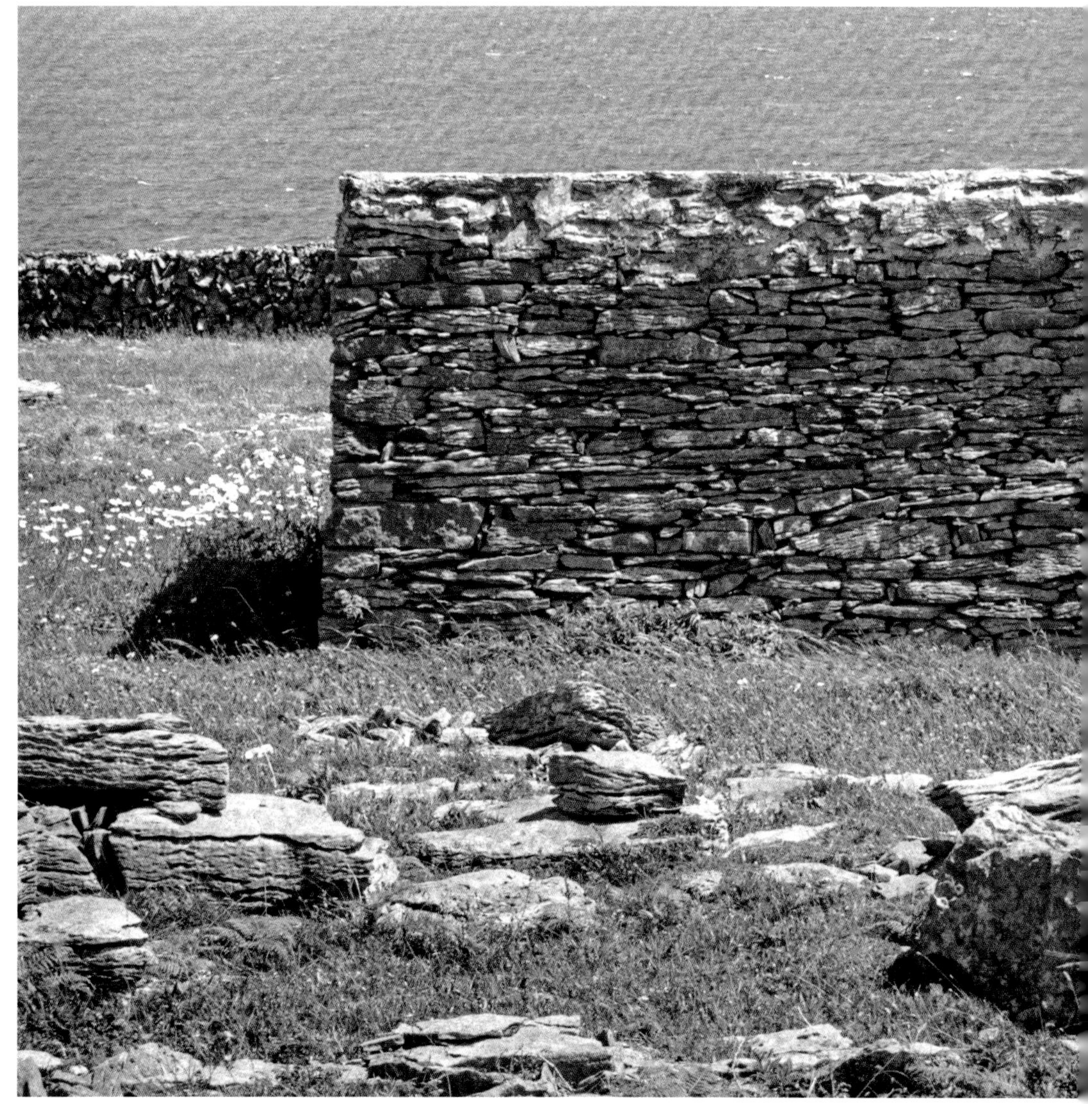

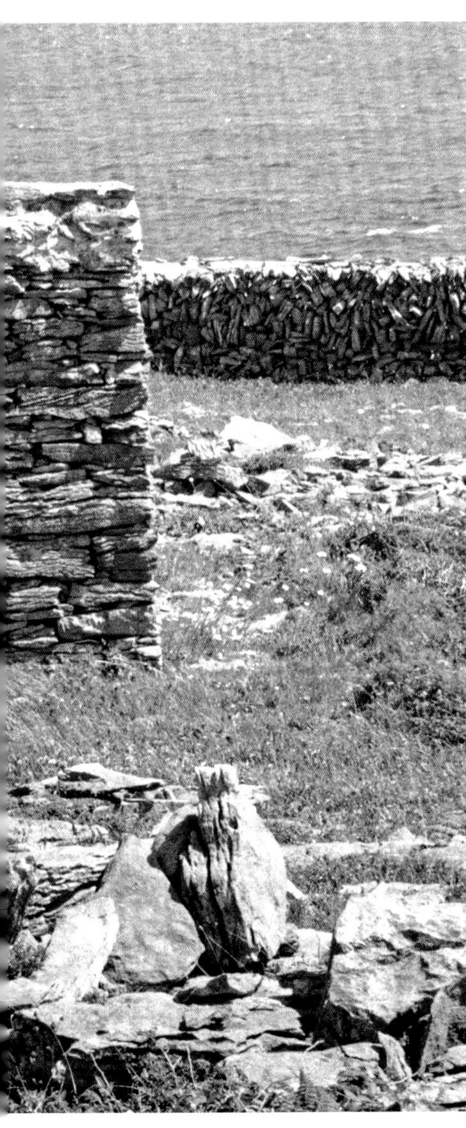

SEAN SCULLY: DRAWING UNTO ARAN

Liliy and I arrived on Inis Oírr in a tiny plane on 20 June 2005, with the intention of staying a week. I invited my class of students from the Art Academy in Munich, and to my amazement they all came, with the exception of one ex-dancer, now a painter, who was in a custody battle back in Munich over the domicile fate of his small son.

Liliy and I stayed at a sweet small hotel called Tigh Ruairi – in English, The Strand House. The students stayed in a hostel nearby, lying in rows on the floor intimately side by side. I never wanted to see where they were staying in case it was terrible, which would have made me upset, so I pretended to myself that it was a kind of hotel. In any case, their faces told me they were happy.

I thought it would be interesting for them to move for one week from the centre of Europe to its very edge. From a major city of profound history and sophistication, where every main boulevard has a museum, to a small island that remains elemental. Where they could look at the materials of the world without embellishment. Where grass is grass and is not cut every month. Where stone is stone and is not polished.

After a few days the students seemed bewitched. They all looked, every one of them, as if fairies had been dancing on their faces in the night. And in the day they were ready to believe that the wind carried voices and the ground was made of magic stones. That proved to me that the hostel, or the hotel as I liked to think of it, was a special place. So I was happy.

The staircases of our modest hotel were decorated profusely with tapestries about the size of picnic tables, which depicted utterly bizarre pictures of a rustic, rural, bygone Ireland. A place where people presumably loved to peel potatoes and write poetry in their spare time – and they had plenty of it because everything was so nice. Liliy and I were fascinated by the oddness of these tapestries and thought of them as Art, because as decoration they were surreal. Cottages were brutally woven out of blobs and blocks of thumb-thick green, yellow and russet nylon material, which was stitched in lines, swirls, points and curves to show a mad idea of a virtual place that would be lovely Ireland. But it was seen from the Chinese perspective, since that's where the tapestries were made. We loved the thought of people in a factory in China, perhaps with a view through a grid of windows in a skyscraper, imagining and depicting, in mechanical nylon, a wistfully concocted innocence. A Yeats tower, for example, rendered in material manufactured in China and realized in the imagined Chinese vision of an Ireland that may or may not have existed in the first place. Possibly for a few romantic years some time in the nineteenth century.

Naturally we wanted to buy some. It seemed, however, that the strangeness of the tapestries affected everything that pertained to them. I went with the owner of the hotel – the husband half of the partnership, that is – to a small tourist gift shop they owned next door. He opened it up for me one night and offered me all the examples he didn't want for himself. It turned out he was a collector; and unfortunately every time I wanted one it was the very one he coveted for himself. So it became quite combative in a non-confrontational dreamy tapestry kind of way. Two men arguing in a storeroom in the middle of the night on the very edge of Europe, about ownership of a Chinese vision of their land. I ended up with three. Not my first choices, naturally, but he wouldn't give those to me for love nor money. Two are now in the rooms of friends' children, just to ensure that they grow up with a vivid imagination, and one hangs over my bath in Bavaria. When I lie reading a Turkish author in my hot water I can look up at a nylon place that is not my land.

On our third day, we made a boat trip to Inis Meáin, over the bumpy surface of the Atlantic. Aran is a challenge to us. It is the way things used to be, and the way things are not any longer everywhere else. And the challenge gets progressively stronger as you taste the escalating solitude of Mór, Oírr and Meáin, in that order – Inis Meáin being the most austere. It is less austere than it was a hundred years ago, but is still more so than almost anywhere else in Europe. For years, there was talk of building a jetty so tourist boats could land. By the time the twenty-first century appeared the talk was over: the discussion/argument had been won by the jetty promoters and the jetty built. Now the tourists can come and enjoy the pub by the dock. They could enjoy it before, but now it's easier to get to.

If you find yourself in charge of thirty art students from Munich, as I did, it's a relief to know that on the far side of the island there is a shop where you can buy potato chips – or crisps, as they're called in Ireland – among other delights. We also found a pub. Black, old and beautiful. With one customer. When the students entered, the one customer turned into thirty-one customers. The pub has been there for hundreds of years – or a little less actually, 150 years. I, in my idiocy, asked the barmaid if it was new. First of all it was hot, and I had been clambering over so many stone walls in a weather cocktail of blasting sun and masculine wind that my senses were scattered. Scattered and shattered. Also, I'm always getting lost. Last time I was on the island, ten years ago, I was unable to find this place. I usually find what I'm looking for when I'm in the company of more than just myself. Anyway, at the end of all of this, some of which I foolishly explained to the barmaid, she told me no, it wasn't new. The whole affair probably struck her as weird. Thirty students from Germany and their teacher who was very simple minded. I was, though, old enough to purchase alcohol, so that part was OK, and we were able to make a little business transaction. Without smiles. We went walking all across the islands between the walls. Walls that walk everywhere. Strolling into squares of oddness and rectangles that lurch in song with the lay of the land. A regularity that is not regular. The stone-wall makers tap the stones into place by sound. When that tap taps right, it's found its place with the thousands of other stones that form the barriers and containers marking out the islands. Each stone where it should be and where it will be, in vertical, in diagonal, in horizontal structured style. Handwriting that denies its character, its personality avowing its proletariat modesty. And yet it displays that personality spectacularly and relentlessly in grey on green, field after field after field. Followed by more. A green-grey loneliness bounded.

The walls of Aran are famous. And more than famous, they are mythic. I am not the only one to photograph them. They are glamorous in their greyness, and strange in their lack of known authorship. I nominate them as Art because of their unremitting, austere, repetitive variety. They are functional, but so are wire fences. So is plastic. But these are not plastic. They are the ground made vertical, with drawing. Drawing that is spectacular and self-effacing. Always insisting on its subservience to function – that being to keep the raking wind out and the animals in. So should Art be useless and only ever that? So that its intensity is unfettered? These are walls whose drawing is diagonal, horizontal, vertical in rhythms of silence. In a tiny land where music is sung and played in pubs and in the air daily, these walls are silent. And yet this sculpture is like the music of this place: austere and elemental.

And unlike art made by known artists, we can love them without loving the maker. The ego of the maker is in the wind that blows through the island from every direction. And, besides, these are collaborations by artists who are mostly gone and mostly unremembered. They are monumental yet egoless. A painting by Picasso is emphatically by him. He is everywhere in the ego of the work and its signature. A Rubens painting that is not entirely by him brings the subject of authorship to the point of crisis. Then there is doubt, reassured by connoisseurship constantly at play as we appreciate the parts painted by the master's hand more than the parts that are not. On Aran all this falls away. They are walls, or they are Art, or they are Art as wall. As we wish. The land is bounded but we are free. We look, we see, and the drawing is everywhere and miraculous.

Sean Scully

On page 16: (top) *Maesta*, 1983. Oil on canvas, 243.8 x 304.8 cm; (bottom)
All About, 1985. Oil on canvas, 213.4 x 261.6 cm
On page 17: Long Night, 1985. Oil on canvas, 243.8 x 304.8 cm
On page 34: (top) *Yellow Bar*, 2002. Oil on canvas, 190.5 x 203 cm; (bottom)
Wall of Light Pink, 1998. Oil on canvas, 243.8 x 304.8 cm
On page 35: *Yellow Red Light*, 1996. Oil on canvas, 243.8 x 213.4 cm
On page 90: (top) *Wall of Light Red Day Leaving*, 2006. Oil on linen, 214 x 243.5 cm;
(bottom) *Wall of Light Red Green*, 2006. Oil on canvas, 197 x 232 cm
On page 91: *Shenandoah*, 2006. Oil on canvas, 182 x 214 cm
All works by Sean Scully

First published in 2020 in the United States of America by
Thames & Hudson Inc., 500 Fifth Avenue, New York, New York 10110

www.thamesandhudsonusa.com

Library of Congress Control Number 2019936122

ISBN 978-0-500-54513-3

Printed and bound in China by C&C Offset Printing Co. Ltd